SMASHING SETS

Margaret J. Miller

Exciting Ways to Arrange Quilt Blocks

C&T PUBLISHING INC.

©2000 Margaret Miller
Illustrations ©2000 C&T Publishing, Inc.

Editor: Liz Aneloski
Technical Editor: Stephanie E. Philp
Copy Editor: Steve Cook
Book Designer: Kristen Yenche
Book Production: Nancy Koerner
Production Coordination: Diane Pedersen
Production Assistant: Kirstie L. McCormick
Illustrator: Richard Sheppard
Photographer: Mark Frey
Front Cover: Starmaker Series III by Margaret J. Miller
Published by C&T Publishing, Inc., P.O. Box 1456, Lafayette, California 94549

Attention Teachers: C&T Publishing, Inc. encourages you to use this book as a text for teaching. Contact us at 800-284-1114 or www.ctpub.com for more information about the C&T Teachers Program.

We take great care to ensure that the information included in this book is accurate and presented in good faith, but no warranty is provided nor results guaranteed. Since we have no control over the choice of materials or procedures used, neither the author nor C&T Publishing, Inc. shall have any liability to any person or entity with respect to any loss or damage caused directly or indirectly by the information contained in this book.

Trademarked (™) and Registered Trademarked (®) names are used throughout this book. Rather than use the symbols with every occurrence of a trademark and registered trademark name, we are using the names only in an editorial fashion and to the benefit of the owner, with no intention of infringement.

Library of Congress Cataloging-in-Publication Data

Miller, Margaret J.
      Smashing sets : exciting ways to arrange quilt blocks / Margaret
   Miller.
            p.   cm.
      Includes bibliographical references and index.
      ISBN 1-57120-110-6
      1. Patchwork. 2. Quilting. 3. Patchwork quilts. I. Title.
   TT835 .M5223 2000
   746.46—dc21
                                    00-008346

Printed in Hong Kong
10 9 8 7 6 5 4 3 2 1

CONTENTS

DEDICATION

To my sister, Janet Thompson Freiland, who has been squarely in the middle of my cheering section right from the start . . .

ACKNOWLEDGEMENTS

Many thanks to all the quiltmakers who have so freely given me blocks to put together for them over the years. The challenges they have offered have been exhilarating, energizing, and at times exhausting. Their generosity in loaning their blocks with no hint of how they would ultimately look is most appreciated! Without them, this book would not have been possible.

A special thanks goes to Kathy Sandbach, who worked with me right to the deadline, furiously machine quilting as fast as I could produce the tops and schedule the photo shoots. The magic she works on a quilt top with her style of machine quiltmaking is truly inspirational.

Most of all, thanks to Liz Aneloski, Todd Hensley, and the entire C&T family for their impeccably professional, heartfelt support and encouragement of quiltmakers in general, and quilt book authors in particular!

INTRODUCTION

The seed for this book was probably planted very soon after I realized that quiltmaking was going to be a big part of my life. I was attending a huge quilt show in San Diego in the late 1970s and had sat down to rest for a while to counteract a bad case of visual overload.

While resting, I began people-watching, which I often do whenever I am surrounded by a sea of humanity—in airports, concerts, or anywhere outside the haven of my own home. I noticed people meandering up and down the aisles of quilts, until they got to the aisle at the end of which I was sitting. They started down the aisle, then started to pick up speed! By the time they got to the end of this aisle of quilts, they weren't even looking at what was hung there. Curious, I got up to see which quilts were hanging in that aisle— and sure enough, it was the traditional samplers: three blocks wide by four blocks long. What a shame, I thought—the show-goers weren't even seeing quilts that had taken every bit as much planning and perseverance as the more innovatively designed quilts.

At that moment I began a quest to come up with innovative settings for traditional sampler blocks, something that would make people take a second look at sampler quilts. I didn't want to make hundreds of sampler blocks myself for this purpose, and I wanted to challenge myself to use colors I don't naturally choose. And so I began to solicit blocks from friends and ask for chances to make special quilts for special people. These blocks were made by hundreds of quiltmakers from all over the country and the world. Some groups of blocks were certainly more challenging than others to put together!

This book features the sampler quilts I have made since 1992, along with a few made by quiltmakers I have met along the way. Though some of the quilts appear to be quite complex, they are all based on simple design principles. All unusual angles, for instance, are created by "connecting the dots" of design points assigned on a piece of graph paper, not by using sophisticated drafting tools. Some complexity is added by doing strip piecing before the template is cut out. Compare the line drawings in Chapter Five with the photos of the quilts throughout the book, and you will see how simple the quilt plans really are.

HOW TO USE THIS BOOK

The most important tool you need to make the most of this book is a good attitude: make sure you have a desire to look at traditional sampler blocks with new eyes. From now on, vow to "reach for the unexpected" in any quilt you tackle that is based on traditional blocks. If your goal is to make blocks of a traditional pattern "sing a new song," and make viewers take a second look at your quilt made from them, you are ready to begin!

Peruse this entire book first, to "prime the pump" of your mind and get it in the mode of thinking about sampler blocks in new ways. Next, if you have a set of sampler blocks stashed away, get them out and put them up on your design wall. Keep them in your mind as you review this book, and notice them during the day as the light changes, as the ideas in this book begin to roll around in your head. Then scan the chapters to see which method of reaching for the unexpected appeals to you most. Finally, jump in; design and piece an innovative setting for the blocks on your wall!

Another important guideline is this: do not let thoughts of piecing interfere with the design process! With the streamlined template system explained in Chapter Four and the simple designing process presented in this book, you will find that these quilts only look complex.

If you have lots of loose blocks, remember that you may choose not to use all of them when designing an innovative setting. It is less intimidating to design for three, six, or nine of them (even if you have 12, 15, or more to choose from), especially if you don't really care for all of them! On the other hand, it is an advantage to not be very attached to this first set of blocks with which you try to "reach for the unexpected," because you are more willing to take risks with them! Remember, if your first foray into innovative design doesn't work, there are many charity quilt committees who will gladly accept your quilt top—and you don't even have to sign and date the quilt if you don't consider it successful!

SUPPLIES

Very few supplies are needed to create innovative sampler quilts. Two different piecing processes are presented in Chapter Four, and supplies for each process are listed there. In general, the following simple and readily available supplies are needed for the design and construction process.

DESIGN TOOLS

• **Pencils, eraser:** I use #2 pencils and Pink Pearl® erasers.

• **Graph paper:** A cross-section pad with eight squares per inch will enable you to make a scale drawing of a quilt as large as 64" × 84" on an 8 1/2" × 11" sheet of paper. The heavier blue line printed every inch on the "cross-section pad" enables you to count inches more quickly for the full size drawing.

• **Tracing paper:** This will allow you to experiment with ideas quickly, without the fear of laborious erasing if a design is "going nowhere."

• **Rulers:** Do not use a thick, plexiglas straightedge for pencil design work, because its thickness will cast a shadow which interferes with accuracy and will add to the time it takes to draw any given design. Having both long (12"–18") and short (6") rulers made from thin plastic facilitates speed in design work.

• **Colored paper:** Typing-paper weight is best, but construction paper can be used to make "blanks" to represent quilt blocks on the graph paper page.

• **Adhesives:** Rubber cement, glue stick, and temporary adhesive that comes in a plastic applicator (with cassette refill) are useful.

• **Color wheel:** This is always a good tool to grow more familiar with as you continue your exploration of color choices.

• **Camera with flash capability:** A camera is almost as essential a tool to a quilt designer as the design wall is. Photograph your quilt while it is in progress. You may see things in the photographs that you didn't notice while designing and cutting the pieces for the quilt.

- **Reducing glass:** This helps you evaluate your use of value (the lightness or darkness of your selection of fabrics). It helps you focus on the value, not just the color of the fabrics on your design wall.
- **Idea Book:** Always keep a notebook handy not only to tack down what you have photographed in the "in progress" snapshots you have taken, but also to record the numerous ideas that will pop into your head in the process!
- **Time (to let the design develop):** This may be the most challenging "supply" to acquire. Give yourself time not only to develop the design, but also to live with it on the design wall for a couple days—or even weeks—and get perspective on what you have created. Give yourself permission to "go back to the drawing board" as your design develops! Sometimes you can't see what a given area of a quilt design needs until you see it in living color!
- **Design wall:** This is the most important tool of all. Since we human beings have eyes placed on the front of our heads, rather than under our chins, we can see color and design more efficiently if we see things on a vertical surface, instead of a horizontal one.

SEWING TOOLS
- **Sewing machine:** Be sure it is cleaned and oiled, and has a new, sharp needle.
- **Iron and pressing surface:** These should be within convenient reach of the sewing machine.
- **General notions:** The most essential ones are straight pins, a seam ripper, and thread snippers. Fill several bobbins with neutral color thread before you begin.

CUTTING TOOLS
- **Rotary cutting mat:** It should be large enough to cut strips from folded fabric (at least 24" wide), and new enough so that tracing a line around a freezer-paper template is not a "bumpy," and thus inaccurate, experience.
- **Acrylic rulers:** You will need several: 6" × 24", 15" (or larger) square, and 3" × 18."
- **Rotary cutters:** Use one with a sharp blade for fabric and one with a blade too dull to cut fabric, for paper!

FABRICS
Use good quality, (high thread count), 100% cotton fabrics. Always choose from your own fabric collection before shopping for more. You bought these fabrics because you liked them, so this is a good place to start using them!

Select a run of fabrics which you feel would be a good backdrop to the blocks with which you are working to start with. This run could go from light to dark, or perhaps from warm colors to cool ones (all of which are of a similar value). Choose more fabrics, rather than fewer. Pretend that you are choosing a paint box of colors—you may be "mixing your paints" later by strip piecing or checkerboarding these fabrics. The most important factor is that whatever colors you choose, try to go "all the way up" to the lights, and "all the way down" to the darks in the range of fabrics chosen for the final quilt.

Whatever you choose, pull these fabrics *quickly*, and *don't agonize* over your choices. The basic color theory of this book is "never use two fabrics when you can use twenty"— a freeing place to start.

CHAPTER 1

Getting Started:

GOALS and DEFINITIONS

The theme of this book is "Reach for the Unexpected." This is what I want you to do in arranging traditional (or more recently designed) quilt blocks in innovative settings. First, however, we must create a definition which will facilitate that goal.

To ready your mind for this task, remember the old saying: "If you always do what you've always done, you'll always get what you always got." If you keep this thought uppermost in your mind, you'll reach for the unexpected at every step along the way to create innovative block settings.

Second, this book will help you come up with novel ideas not only for the arrangements of the blocks in the interior of the quilt ("the setting"), but also for the border area of the quilt, which showcases this setting. Don't think about the center of the quilt and the border as two different elements of the quilt, but rather as two areas of the quilt to keep in mind at all times as you develop your design.

Think of the border not as a "fence" necessary to "hold the blocks in," but as an area in which the quilt can come to a gradual, visual close. The border area is a natural extension of the setting of the blocks in the central area of the quilt. Using the techniques in this book, you will try to camouflage where the quilt stops and the border begins.

Some quilts do not need a border treatment in the traditional sense, because they have already come to a visual close merely by the way the blocks have transitioned or by the way the central motif has dissipated by the time the eyes reach the edge of the quilt.

ACQUIRING QUILT BLOCKS TO WORK WITH

Like most quiltmakers, you probably have sets of unassembled blocks stashed away somewhere in the house and, chances are, these are not your favorite blocks. Perhaps you have even forgotten (conveniently) that you have them at all! They may be the blocks you made in your first quilting class (in which case they may be 15" squares with four matching fabrics, as mine were—one print, and three solids that matched exactly the rosebuds in the print!). Or, they may be an odd-numbered set of "Block of the Month" blocks from your quilt guild (and you wish you hadn't won that month!) Or, they may be a set of friendship blocks that made you wonder about the friendship when you saw the workmanship that came back. . .

Whatever blocks you have, take them out and look at them with fresh eyes. If you really don't care for them, so much the better—then you'll be more willing to take risks with how you put them together! And after all, if the results don't please you, you can send the quilt top off to your guild charity project; the ultimate recipient won't have to know that you made this one!

If you don't have any blocks on hand, talk to your quilting friends. Someone is bound to have a set of blocks she *knows* she will never put together and you will eliminate her guilt about not doing so by asking for them. Whether you promise to give her the quilt top once finished is personal preference, or perhaps a point of negotiation. Regardless, make sure that the block donor gives you these blocks with "no strings attached"—no expectations, no restrictions.

Once you have played with a set of blocks, you may wish to progress to quilt tops which were never finished because they lack a border. If, horror of horrors, you didn't buy enough of one of the fabrics from the center to make the standard "three bands of fabric around the quilt," don't worry! As you explore your new "reach for the unexpected" attitude toward quilt design, you will find that the border need not have anything in common with the center area of the quilt, either in fabric choices or color.

PREPARATION OF SAMPLER OR FRIENDSHIP BLOCKS

The first step in working with any set of blocks is to put them up on the design wall. It is crucial to keep your quilt in progress on the design wall at all times, beginning right now! Ideas for setting the blocks may occur to you when you least expect it, often when you are not consciously working out a plan for them. If your blocks are not up on the wall where you can catch sight of them at different times of the day (so you see them in different levels of light) and from different angles, you will not be as receptive to this unconscious flow of ideas.

BORDERING EACH BLOCK

If the blocks you plan to work with were made by different quiltmakers, you are probably dealing with varying levels of craftsmanship. You may have various-size blocks, and they may not all be truly square. Further, the colors and patterns may not be unified, especially if no theme was established to begin with.

To compensate for these differences, add a narrow border (about 1" finished) around each block. Cut 1³/₄"-wide strips across the grain of the fabric. Be sure that the fold is on grain when your selvages are aligned; then, cut strips perpendicular to the folds and selvages. Sew these strips "willy nilly" (without mitering corners and without squaring up blocks to begin with) to the edges of sampler blocks. Press seam allowances toward border strips.

You can then place your own square template onto this bordered block and be sure that you have a truly square block to put into the quilt. You will be amazed at how misshapen a block can be and still not be noticeably crooked in the final quilt once it has been surrounded with this narrow border of fabric.

What fabric should you choose for such a border? The function of the block border is not to only compensate for varying levels of craftsmanship, but also to separate each block from its neighbor (or from its background) enough that it doesn't matter that the set of

Cut 1³/₄"-wide strips across the grain of the fabric.

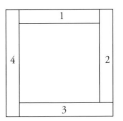

Sew strips to the edges of the sampler blocks.

blocks is unrelated in color or design. Decide first if you are going to use the block border to enhance the design of a given block and enhance the colors used therein, or if you are choosing a block border because it will be the unifying element in a set of unrelated blocks.

Fabrics which are medium to dark in value are a good choice or you can use a stripe (either crosswise or lengthwise along the border strip). Flip through the photos of quilts in this book to get a feeling for the range of possible choices for block border fabrics.

Whether you border all the blocks or only some of them, remember to keep your blocks on the wall at all times. Once the border of the block is sewn and pressed, put it back on the design wall. Play with various arrangements of the blocks during this border-adding process, even though you haven't a clue as to what you will do with the area behind or around the blocks. This does not mean that all traditional blocks should be bordered before being put into a contemporary sampler.

MARION'S FRIENDS I
56" × 56"
Margaret J. Miller
Woodinville, Washington
1999. Machine quilted by
the author. Collection of
Marion Shelton Harlan,
Everett, Washington.

Note that two sizes of quilt
blocks were used; some were
six inches square, others were
eight inches square. By putting
borders around only the smaller blocks, and alternating six
inch and eight inch square
blocks, a pleasing block
arrangement was developed.
Note further that a blue fabric
was used to border the corner
blocks, while a medium pink
print draws the center blocks
together.

STARMAKER SERIES III
65" × 65"
Margaret J. Miller
Woodinville, Washington, 1998.
Machine quilted by Barbara Ford,
Deming, Washington.
Collection of Mary E. Hales,
Mount Vernon, Washington.

There are borders around the eight blocks offset around the center, but the corner blocks, which are smaller than those in the center, are borderless. Notice that the border-less blocks form a more effective corner treatment because they are significantly different in presentation from the blocks in the center.

WORKING TO SCALE WITH COLORED-PAPER BLANKS

All of the steps of this process are designed to keep you from agonizing about any given stage. The number one cause of agonizing for quiltmakers comes from trying to make too many decisions at one time. In order to eliminate agonizing at this stage about "what block goes where," make colored-paper blanks to represent each quilt block *with its attached border*. Using rubber cement, adhere a sheet of eight-squares-per-inch graph paper to a sheet of colored paper.

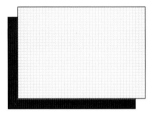

Adhere graph paper to colored paper with rubber cement.

Cut out colored-paper squares to represent your quilt blocks. Use the graph paper lines as a guide, using a scale of one square on the graph paper equaling one square inch of fabric. A twelve-inch quilt block with its border added would measure 14" across. The colored-paper blank which represents that block would be 14 squares by 14 squares ($1^3/4$" × $1^3/4$").

To cut many blanks at once, use a rotary cutter. Cut on the graph paper lines across the paper—that is, cut every 14 graph paper squares if you are making blanks which represent 14" quilt blocks—but stop about a half inch from the edge of the paper. All the strips are held in place by the uncut edge of the paper. Then, cross cut these strips every 14 squares to create the blanks.

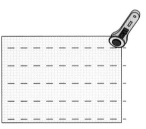

Cut on the graph paper lines across the paper, stopping about $1/2$" from the edge of the paper.

You will create innovative arrangements of your quilt blocks by playing with these paper squares (colored side up) on a blank piece of graph paper. Once you find an arrangement of the squares (quilt blocks) that is pleasing, glue them in place and complete your design by drawing design lines between and around them on the graph paper. By using colored-paper blanks, you will not be distracted by the color or design of individual quilt blocks. Blanks also make the process of designing for more than one size of block in the same quilt much easier.

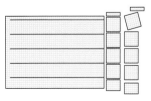

Cross cut the strips to create the blanks.

Chapter 2

WORKING *from the* INSIDE OUT

In this chapter you will experiment with various arrangements of quilt blocks keeping in mind that the goal is to reach for the unexpected in the arrangement of your blocks. Make yourself a supply of 14 squares by 14 squares (or 8 squares by 8 squares, if you prefer) colored paper blanks (see page 11) so you can practice the various arrangements presented, and glue in place the ones that appeal to you. As you play with these arrangements, your own unique block plan may emerge, and you'll want plenty of blanks on hand so you can glue all plans down for future reference.

By placing your bordered blocks edge to edge and offsetting them from each other either horizontally or vertically, you will be able to get more blocks into a single quilt top than you could if you had to separate each pair with a sashing strip. There are various arrangements these offset blocks could form on the quilt surface. We will present arrangements first for blocks used as squares, then for blocks on point.

BLOCKS AS SQUARES

COLUMNS OF BLOCKS

Columns can be horizontal, vertical, or placed on the diagonal across the quilt. The columns of blocks could be relatively straight, or undulating. If the columns of blocks are vertical, the blocks at the top of each column could be on the same graph paper line, or on a different one to create even more variety.

A variation on blocks offset to form horizontal rows is to create a "serpentine" pathway of blocks across the quilt. To determine if your arrangement is balanced, squint at your block layout and notice not only the path of blocks, but the spaces in between the successive layers (rows) of offset blocks.

Horizontal rows of blocks.

Vertical columns of blocks.

Blocks placed diagonally.

SUNBONNET SUE GOES BOWLING

79" × 87"

Margaret J. Miller
Woodinville, Washington, 1993.
Machine quilted by
the author. Blocks by quilting group
"Monday Night Bowling League,"
Seattle, Washington.

This quilt is a good example of a serpentine pathway of blocks. Note that the blocks are different shapes and sizes; by creating a colored paper blank for each bordered block, it was relatively easy to create the pathway of blocks on a blank sheet of graph paper.

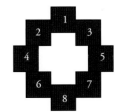

Circular arrangement of blocks.

Once the serpentine block pathway was determined in the quilt above, I drew the "open box" image behind each block. The edge of the quilt was determined by counting eight graph paper squares beyond the outermost blocks on all four sides of the quilt. The flying geese border was then drawn between the blocks and the perimeter.

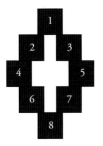

Oval arrangement of blocks.

CIRCULAR AND OVAL ARRANGEMENTS

Creating a halo of blocks around either an open area or a focus motif in the center of a quilt is a very versatile design device.

Note in the diagrams to the right that the second and third blocks are offset to the side and down from the top of the center block and the fourth and fifth blocks are not only set off to the side, but also placed *underneath* the second and third blocks. This is what helps you form a circle, not a pyramid, of blocks!

To create an oval rather than a circular arrangement of blocks, place blocks two and three to the side and under block number one. Or, if you have more than eight blocks, "stack" them between the three blocks at the top and bottom of the oval arrangement.

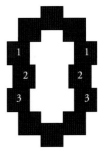

Stack blocks between the three blocks at the top and bottom.

KERRY'S HEARTS I
70" × 70"
Margaret J. Miller
Woodinville, Washington,
1997. Machine quilted by
Roxanne Carter, Mukilteo,
Washington. Collection of
Kerry I. Smith, Bainbridge
Island, Washington.

Note that some of the blocks
were offset to form a circle of
blocks around the five blocks
in the center. The blocks offset to form rounded corners
formed a graceful finish to
this gentle quilt. To get such
a large circle of blocks, note
carefully which blocks are
offset to the side of the previous block and which are offset to the side and under
their neighbors.

MEDORA ON MY MIND

68" × 64"

Margaret J. Miller

Woodinville, Washington, 1999. Machine quilted by Kathy Sandbach, Volcano, California. Collection of Phyllis Bogart, Melnor, North Dakota. Blocks made by quiltmakers attending Quilting in the Badlands 1998, a retreat held in Medora, North Dakota.

Notice that there are two blocks in the center of the quilt and a "broken circle" formed by offset blocks around them. One of the blocks in the set destined for this quilt was made up of two of the tree blocks, side by side. I unsewed the center seam and made more tree blocks to "sprinkle" throughout this quilt, hence the broken circle. The blocks are not offset symmetrically, but a circular feeling was developed nonetheless.

ROAD TO CALIFORNIA

88" × 101"

Margaret J. Miller

Woodinville, Washington, 1995.
Hand quilted by Catherine Gilbert. Collection of Carolyn M. Reese, Montclair, California.

The challenge was to place a very large number of blocks into a single quilt. Note that the outer framing circle of blocks is actually formed with two quilt blocks side by side or one above the other. To help define the circle, the borders on the outermost blocks are darker than on the inner ones.

JEKYLL ISLAND COMPASS

55½" × 67"

Margaret J. Miller Woodinville, Washington, 1997. Machine quilted by Kathy Sandbach, Volcano, California. Collection of Georgia Quilt Council, care of Jean C. Wolfe, Marietta, Georgia. Blocks made by quiltmakers attending Jekyll Island Quilt Retreat, Jekyll Island Georgia, 1996.

A circular arrangement of offset blocks can be made to look oval by the design lines around it. In this quilt, the eight largest blocks form a circle around the Mariner's Compass block in the middle. However, since the design lines forming borders around the center block are not parallel to it, and since the outer perimeter of the quilt is a rectangle and not a square, at first glance you might think that this is an oval arrangement of blocks.

STARFISH ON JEKYLL ISLAND
70" × 82"
Margaret J. Miller
Woodinville, Washington, 1998.
Machine quilted by Kathy Sandbach, Volcano, California. Collection of Georgia Quilt Council, care of Jean C. Wolfe, Marietta, Georgia. Blocks made by quiltmakers attending Jekyll Island Quilt Retreat, Jekyll Island Georgia, 1996.

This is an example of a spiral arrangement with smaller blocks in the center and larger ones on the outer whorls of the spiral. The spiral ends with a small block on the lower left side of the quilt.

Note how unrelated in color and design the blocks are in this quilt and how effectively the borders used around each block allow the eye to move smoothly from one block to the next. No border was added around the ship block, as it arrived with its own coral border!

SPIRAL ARRANGEMENTS

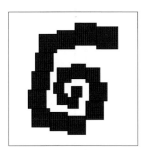

Creating spiral arrangements of offset blocks is another variation on this circular theme. In order to create a pleasing spiral arrangement of blocks it is important to pay attention not only to the pathway of blocks but also to the spaces between the successive pathways.

If your blocks are various sizes, you can add more visual complexity to the spiral by consciously grading the block sizes from the center out. For example, you could place the smallest block in the center and gradually work out to the largest one. Or, by putting the largest block in the center and working out to the smallest one, you might create the illusion that your blocks are emerging from a point very far behind the quilt surface.

Even if all your blocks are the same size, if they are small you can create this gradation in block size by increasing the width of the border you put around each block.

HEART SHAPE PATHWAYS OF BLOCKS

This is an especially effective arrangement for a quilt with a sentimental message. The open area inside the heart shape can be used for people to write messages or sign their names.

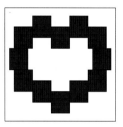

Heart shape arrangements of offset blocks can take on various configurations, depending on how much or how little the blocks are offset from each other.

GOOD WISHES FOR PAM
62" × 69"
Margaret J. Miller
Woodinville, Washington, 1994.
Machine quilted by the author.
Collection of Pamela A. Anderson, Mount Vernon, Washington. The cat appliqués were designed by Linda Peterson of Great Falls, Montana, for her pattern "Sampler and Friends: The Cat Quilt."

This quilt was purposely created with a lot of open space for friends to write words of hope and good cheer to support Pam during her high-dose chemotherapy for breast cancer. The appliquéd cat shapes helped fill out an otherwise straightforward design.

MARION'S STOREFRONTS
67" × 72"
Margaret J. Miller
Woodinville, Washington, 1991.
Hand quilted by the Amish.
Collection of Marion Shelton Harlan, Everett, Washington.
Blocks made by Marion's quilting friends, block designed by Carol C. Porter, Everett, Washington.

The blocks are in the same arrangement as those in Pam's quilt (above); however, once the blocks were in the heart-shaped arrangement, an additional border was drawn around each block. The borders are purposely overlapped; this became a place to practice "transparency" in fabric choices.

EMPTY SPOOLS
AT ASILOMAR I
60" × 72"
Margaret J. Miller
Woodinville, Washington
1995. Quilted by Kathy
Sandbach, Volcano,
California. Collection of
Gayle Wells, Moraga,
California. Blocks made by
some of the 53 teachers who
taught during the first ten
years of the Empty Spools
Seminars at Asilomar.

Notice how the blocks
invade the pieced border on
all four sides; in essence, the
border became the "support"
which visually held those
blocks in place.

OFFSETTING BLOCKS IN NO SPECIAL ARRANGEMENT

This arrangement is very useful if you have a large number of blocks of varying sizes and you want to get them all into a single quilt. This was true of *Empty Spools at Asilomar I* (above), one of three quilts for which blocks had been sent from a group of 53 teachers of quiltmaking. Note how unrelated in color and design the set of blocks in each of these quilts is, and how the narrow border around each block allows them all to exist comfortably in the same quilt!

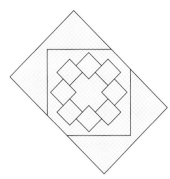

BLOCKS ON POINT

For blocks on point, you could consider similar offset arrangements to those described for square blocks above. However, since blocks on point take up almost half again as much horizontal and vertical space as square blocks, not as many blocks will end up in a single quilt.

USING GRAPH PAPER ON POINT

If all the blocks in your quilt can be placed on point, you can use your graph paper on point to create your design. This was the approach used in designing Virginia Avery's Sisterhood Quilt.

This means that the horizontal and vertical lines in your quilt (such as the top, bottom, and side edges) will actually be drawn corner to corner on the graph paper. This often means you have to add graph paper to complete the drawing of the quilt. See page 64 for how to add sheets of graph paper quickly, easily, and accurately.

If this approach feels too confusing to you, follow the guidelines for designing quilts with both blocks as squares and blocks on point in the same piece (page 21).

When working with graph paper on point, place the drawing in front of you so that you are looking at the quilt as it will be seen on the wall (or on the bed). Don't try to work with the paper straight and your quilt drawing on point!

THIS PURPLE SISTER SLEEPS WARM
70" × 65"
Margaret J. Miller
Woodinville, Washington, 1995.
Quilted by Linda Gunby, Poulsbo, Washington. Collection of Virginia Avery, Port Chester, New York. Blocks made by six-member friendship group Sisterhood of the Purple.

USING GRAPH PAPER STRAIGHT

To create a colored-paper blank to represent the block on point, adhere colored paper to graph paper with rubber cement. Using the graph paper lines as a guide, cut out one square which is either 12 squares on a side (to represent the block alone) or 14 squares on a side (to represent the block with a narrow border attached).

Place this square, colored side up, onto a glued graph-paper/colored-paper set so that the opposite corners of the block line up on a single horizontal and a single vertical line.

When working with graph paper to create scale drawings of full-size quilts, it is essential that all design points are at an intersection of two graph paper lines. After all, each square of the graph paper represents one square inch of fabric. To find a given design point when making the full-size quilt, one needs to be able to count inches. Note that the corners of the square block placed on point don't coincide exactly with crossing graph paper lines.

Therefore, blocks on point will require slightly wider borders around them so that their (finished) size can be drawn accurately using intersecting graph paper lines on the scale drawing.

Place a pencil dot at the juncture of graph paper lines closest to each corner of your colored-paper square.

Repeat these pencil dots to create new cutting lines. Using these, you will cut out accurate colored-paper blanks to represent blocks on point. These blanks can now be used in an on-point orientation on graph paper with lines horizontally and vertically in front of you. The corners of the on-point blocks will always line up at the intersection of two graph paper lines.

Blocks on point can be arranged in columns, spirals, ovals, or in no special pattern, just like straight blocks. However, keep in mind that blocks on point take up more space in the quilt, so you may not be able to get as many blocks into a quilt surface; likewise, a quilt with blocks on point will be larger than a quilt with blocks as squares in the same arrangement. For example, if you used eight blocks as squares to form a circle and placed the edge of the quilt four inches beyond the outermost blocks, your quilt would measure 40" × 40". If those same eight blocks were placed on point in a circular, offset arrangement with the same perimeter allowances, you would create a quilt at least 42" × 42".

COMBINING STRAIGHT AND ON-POINT BLOCKS

You are more likely to be combining square blocks and blocks on point in a single quilt than you are to use all blocks on point in a single quilt. The combination of both shapes is actually more refreshing than either shape alone. If you are designing with both types of block, straight and on point, make your colored-paper blanks out of different colored papers so you can easily distinguish the two types.

Place the square on point lining up opposite corners of the block on a horizontal and vertical line.

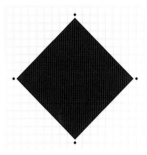

Place a pencil dot on the lines closest to each corner.

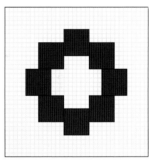

Blocks as squares

Blocks on point

CORNUCOPIA

70" × 94"

Kathleen Moorhead Johnson
Alexander, North Dakota,
1996. Blocks made over
years while teaching basic
quiltmaking from Laura
Nownes' and Diana
McClun's book *Quilts!
Quilts!! Quilts!!!* in her area.

Kathy had quite an extensive
set of sampler blocks after
teaching her basic quiltmaking class numerous times.
She successfully combined
both blocks straight and
blocks on point. Note that
her approach was to "float"
them on a background,
organized by the long corner
to corner diagonals. To
design this quilt, she used
colored paper blanks to represent each block, as
described on page 21.

SPECIAL MESSAGES

65" × 65"

Margaret J. Miller

Woodinville, Washington, 1998.

Collection of Cathie I. Hoover, Modesto, California.

Blocks made and assembled in less than three weeks by four of Cathie's quilting friends to bring her luck and comfort during surgery for breast cancer.

This quilt is another example of combining straight and on-point blocks; forty percent of the blocks in this quilt are the large (12″ square) ones; the rest of the quilt is made up of six inch blocks and variations on the two blocks from this set which were rail fence-style designs. The latter were converted into background areas for the central medallion.

STARMAKER SERIES I

58" × 39"

Margaret J. Miller

Woodinville, Washington, 1998. Quilted by Marty Kutz, Sedro Woolley, Washington. Collection of Mary E. Hales, Mount Vernon, Washington.

This blocks were made by Mary's employees and friends to thank her for her many kindnesses during the ten years she owned The Quilt Shop in Stanwood, Washington. This quilt began with only four blocks; one rectangular one in the center, two smaller square ones on point, and one square block that was cut corner to corner to form the east-west staging for the center block. This grouping is set off entirely by blocks on point.

THE BLOCK LINKING NETWORK

There is a two-fold key to successful presentation of sampler blocks which are not connected by design lines: first, camouflage where the quilt stops and the border begins, and second, use some kind of graphic mechanism in the background that seems to support the blocks in place. Without this mechanism, the quilt looks like you might as well have appliquéd the blocks onto a single fabric background.

In the two Empty Spools at Asilomar quilts below, for example, note that there are horizontal and vertical stripes in the background "behind" the blocks; note further that these stripes go beyond the center of the quilt into the border.

EMPTY SPOOLS
AT ASILOMAR III

72" × 81"

Margaret J. Miller
Woodinville, Washington, 1995.
Machine quilted by Kathy
Sandbach, Volcano, California.
Collection of Diana McClun,
Walnut Creek, California. Blocks
made by some of the 53 teachers who taught during the first
ten years of the Empty Spools
Seminars at Asilomar.

EMPTY SPOOLS
AT ASILOMAR II

60" × 72"

Margaret J. Miller
Woodinville, Washington, 1995.
Machine quilted by Kathy Sandbach,
Volcano, California.
Collection of Suzanne Cox,
Kenwood, California.
See caption above

THE BLOCK AND BLANK APPROACH— SOME "LOOSENING UP" EXERCISES

This section will help you take a fresh approach to the settings for traditional quilt blocks. The principles presented here will be referred to numerous times throughout this book. The key to working in this section is to not let thoughts of piecing interfere with the design process! You will see that piecing these innovative quilts is not difficult when you use the template approach described in Chapter Four (page 63)—so let your imagination soar!

With this approach, instead of starting with colored-paper blanks, start with photocopies of actual quilt blocks. Make at least six photocopies of Appendix A, page 91. Choose three different patchwork patterns (A, B, and C) and glue them (each layout in the center of a single piece of graph paper) as in the configurations at right:

Draw a pencil line around the layouts (indicated by dotted line at right) so that it looks like a nine block quilt, and label them Layout A and Layout B as shown.

Place a piece of tracing paper over each layout, and transfer only corner marks and the letter of the layout you are working with onto the tracing paper. You are going to design an interesting setting for each set of blocks by adding design lines to the blank spaces. Remember that your goal is to reach for the unexpected; your goal is not to add as many lines to the blank blocks as there are in the glued ones. You are creating a *setting* for these blocks that sets them off and presents them well. Don't be afraid of mixing nine-patch and four-patch patterns in the same layout.

The first step in creating an innovative setting for the quilt blocks already in place is to look for design points to connect, and design lines to extend. This often leads to a fairly predictable outcome (see illustrations below).

To reach for the unexpected in creating a setting for these traditional quilt blocks, try one or more of the following approaches.

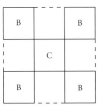

LAYOUT A

LAYOUT B

Letters A, B, and C represent three different patchwork patterns (they may be four-patch and nine-patch patterns mixed).

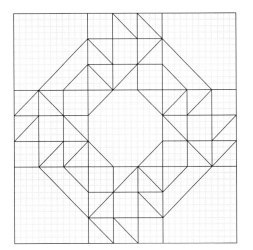

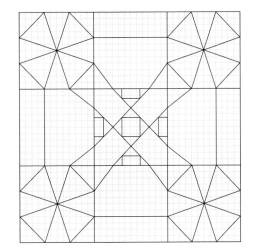

CHANGE THE ANGLE

One way to create an interesting setting for these blocks is to add lines that *change the angle*. When you flip through a book of patchwork patterns, especially the chapters on nine-patch and four-patch patterns, there are two angles that predominate—the 90 degree angle, which is the corner of a square, and the 45 degree angle, which is the point of a right triangle.

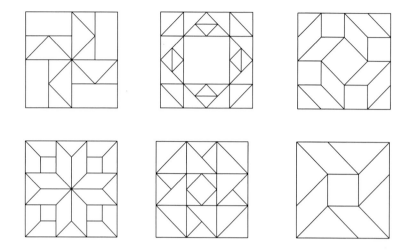

Blocks with 45 and 90 degree angles

Whenever you incorporate some other angle besides 90 or 45 degrees, you create a softness in the blocks' presentation; furthermore, you can introduce either the feeling of curves and "roundedness" in the quilt, or a "radiating" quality, even though there is no curved-seam piecing involved. Look how the character of our sample layouts changes with the addition of lines at a different angle.

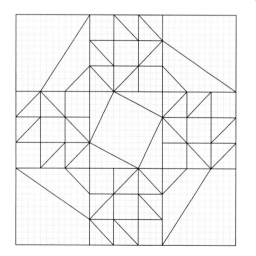

Sample layout with angled lines added.

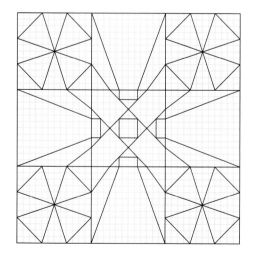

Sample layout with angled lines added.

BUILDING
COMMUNITY II

72" × 72"

Louise Dressen
Kirkland, Washington, 1997.
Hand quilted by members
(quilters and non-quilters
alike!) of the Holy Spirit
Lutheran Church, Kirkland,
Washington. Collection of
Wondem and Lemlen
Dessalegne, Bellevue,
Washington.

This quilt is a good example of the "rounded" feeling that design lines at a different angle can create. Note that the line dividing the purple medallion background fabric and the white in the corner is at a 45 degree angle to the sides, but look at the softness that is created by the design line which separates the teal and purple fabrics.

CAMOUFLAGE WHERE ONE BLOCK STOPS AND ITS NEIGHBOR BEGINS

Look for unexpected design points to connect. Try to create shapes that cross the lines separating one block from its neighbor. Notice how this opens up the possibility of camouflaging where the center block stops and the four adjoining blocks begin.

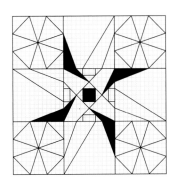

Create shapes that cross the block lines.

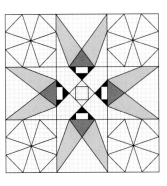

This process is most obvious when we create lines to enhance the center open block in the layout.

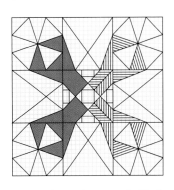

Create shapes that cross the block lines.

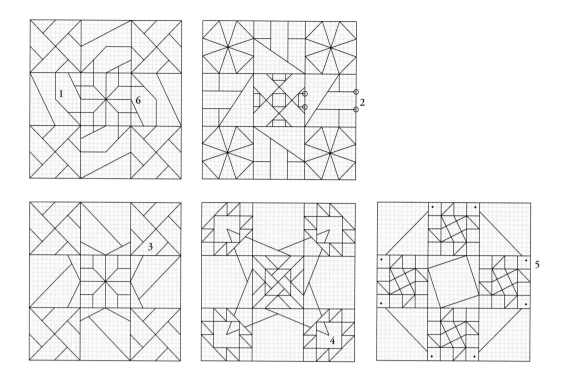

When looking for design points to connect to change the angle, don't restrict yourself to design points at the edge of the blocks, or in their corners. Consider also:

1. the middle of the neighboring block;
2. the same design point on the opposite side of the block;
3. the design points one-third or one-quarter of the way along the edge of the block, even though no design line begins or ends there;
4. the middle of a shape in the next block;
5. a point one or two inches diagonally from the corner of a shape;
6. Design lines may cross the block line from the "empty" block into the given block. Let the shape created by this line end at a shape within the patchwork block, rather than the edge of the block itself.

Remember to make sure that all design points are at the intersection of two graph paper lines. If you are creating an unusual angle and it is not obvious what design points you are using to create it, draw little circles around them so it will be easy to create your full-size templates.

You can also change the angle around the block grouping in a couple of effective ways. In the early days of sampler quilts, a standard approach was to add strips of three different fabrics around the block grouping, with each strip a different width and the four corners mitered. To reach for the unexpected, choose design points along the perimeter of the quilt which will create gradually widening border strips instead of parallel ones.

The border for Linda Gunby's sisterhood quilt, page 30, was designed this way after the plan for the blocks in the center was far enough along that I could determine that

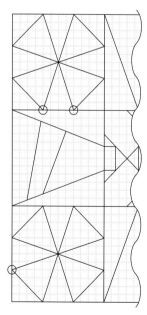

Draw circles around design points that create unusual angles.

the edge of the quilt would be two inches beyond the outermost blocks. Note that the lines creating this "cockeyed nine-patch" in the corners are interrupted by the outermost blocks north, south, east and west on this quilt.

Selecting design points along the edge of the quilt, and connecting them to each other and to the point at the center of the quilt using interrupted lines also changes the angle effectively. The lines will be interrupted by the blocks already arranged in the interior of the quilt. This approach creates the illusion that the spirit of the quilt is exploding, in the form of ribbons or rays of light radiating from its center area.

The radiating ribbons approach was used in *Starmaker Series IV*. Note that the ribbons were further subdivided; the orange ones feature strip piecing that ranges from lighter to darker strips. Any single one of the orange fabrics in that large a space would have been too much orange! The blue ribbons were divided down the middle so that the striped fabric could be cut on the bias to form the chevron design.

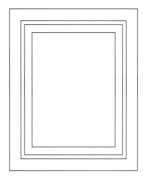

Border seams parallel to the edges of the quilt.

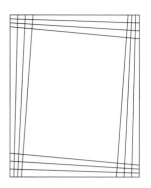

Seam line dividing two border strips is two units from the edge on one side of the quilt, four units from the same edge on the opposite side.

STARMAKER SERIES IV
65" × 65"
Margaret J. Miller
Woodinville, Washington, 1998.
Machine quilted by Patsi Hanseth, Mount Vernon, Washington.
Collection of Mary E. Hales, Mount Vernon, Washington.
Blocks for this and four other quilts in the series made with love and gratitude for Mary by teachers and employees of The Quilt Shop in Stanwood, Washington.

THE ASYMMETRICAL APPROACH

Don't create the same design "north and south" that you do "east and west." Likewise, don't do the same design in all four corners when the "given" blocks are in a north-south-east-west position. This is one approach that will force you to reach for the unexpected. Some people find it difficult to make themselves take the "asymmetrical approach." If you are one of these, keep trying to search for asymmetry; you might be delightfully surprised at the results.

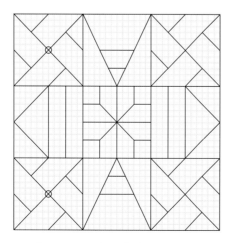

One design in north-south blocks, similar but different designs in east-west blocks.

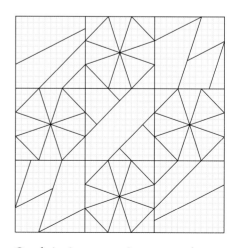

One design in two opposite corners and a different design in the other two corners.

An even simpler way to create this motion is to start with asymmetrical quilt block patterns. Traditional patchwork patterns have one-way or two-way symmetry. If you can place a line on the block, and the pattern is the same on either side of that line, you have one-way symmetry. If a block has two-way symmetry, you can place two crossing lines on it and it will have identical parts on either side of both of these lines.

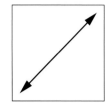

Shorthand way of expressing direction of blocks for one-way (top) and two-way (bottom) symmetry.

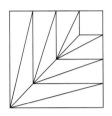   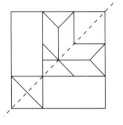   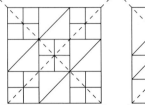   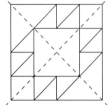

One-way symmetry   Two-way symmetry (directional)

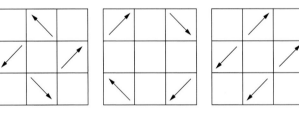   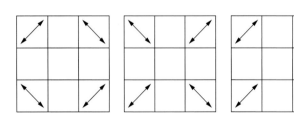

A few ways of positioning one-way symmetrical blocks.   A few ways of positioning two-way symmetrical blocks.

Another way to use asymmetry to add motion to a group of blocks is to break up the blank space in an asymmetrical way. This can create the illusion of "spinning" in a set of blocks checkerboarded with blank spaces in a quilt top.

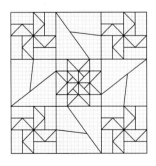

Break up the blank space asymmetrically.

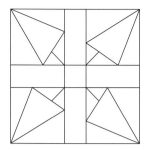

Triangle fills the block.

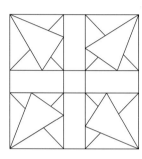

Two "free" corners connected with an interrupted line.

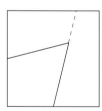

Seam lines which are extensions of existing design lines are easier to piece.

Sometimes you create a more pleasant design by connecting the point with some significant design point nearby. In this example, the corner appears mitered, a good design finish.

PRINCIPLE OF INTERRUPTED LINES

This is perhaps the most dramatic way to reach for the unexpected in the design for your block setting. This technique will bring a three-dimensional look to the two-dimensional surface. In the corner blocks of the example at left, the triangle appears to fill the block adequately. But look what happens when we connect the two "free" corners: these can still be connected by a continuous line or, perhaps more effectively, with an interrupted line—a line that is interrupted by the triangular shape that is already in place.

Notice that with the interrupted line drawn onto the block, the triangle appears closer to the viewer than it did without the interrupted diagonal line.

The principle of interrupted line is one I use as often as I can; as you look at the line drawings in Chapter Five (page 68), you will see countless examples of this. One way to create an interrupted line is to look for design points not at the edge of shapes to connect, but in the interiors of those shapes.

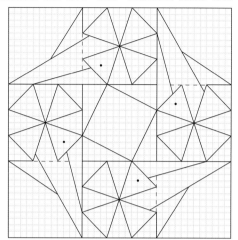

Some of the lines at the edge of the original blocks have been changed to dashed lines. They are now seam lines, not design lines. This helps camouflage where one block stops and its neighbor begins.

PRINCIPLE OF BENT LINES

Yet another possibility is to connect two design points, not with a straight line, but with one which changes angle abruptly at some arbitrary point in the block. (See drawings, page 28). Though you are not to let thoughts of piecing interfere with the design process, remember that whenever you have a point coming out into an open area, you must add a seam line in order to piece that point into the background.

On your scale drawing, make this seam line a dashed line, to distinguish seam lines from design lines. Do not add these dashed seam lines until the designing is complete.

It is usually easier to piece such a point if you extend one of the seam lines that created that point in the first place; however, you may decide to create some other angle when connecting that "jutting" point, either with the corner of the block or with some other design point at the edge of an adjoining block. Sometimes the dashed seam line creates an unexpected interesting shape or miters a corner in an unusual way and becomes a design line after all!

The combinations of these design choices are endless. I encourage you to continue to play with the block and blank layouts you worked with in this chapter and to come up with multiple innovative settings which don't look anything like each other. The beauty of using tracing paper for this exercise is that you can collect multiple successful design approaches; however, if the design you are working on isn't going anywhere, throw away

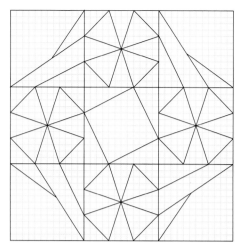

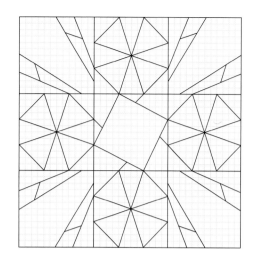

Block grouping setting gives a rounded feeling.

Same block grouping with radiating feeling to the setting.

that tracing paper, reach for a fresh one, and start over! There's no laborious "erasing time" in this process!

Challenge yourself to come up with opposing design approaches with any given layout. For example, if one design seems "rounded," try to create another one for the same block layout that has a "radiating" feeling to it. Be sure to experiment with asymmetrical treatments: design two opposite corners one way, the other two another; design "north and south" one way, "east and west" another. Or, make one design in two adjacent corners (or middle blocks), another design in the other two. Perhaps you will do the same design in three spaces, and a different one in the fourth. And so on . . .

POSITIONING THE QUILT WITHIN THE PERIMETER—AN EXTENSION OF THE "BLOCK AND BLANK" APPROACH

The process of designing a border setting for a set of blocks is less threatening if you realize that the block and blank approach can be applied to the space around the block grouping, between the blocks and the perimeter of the quilt. The perimeter is the edge of the quilt where the binding is attached.

The first step is to define that space and think about how many ways an arrangement of blocks can be positioned within the perimeter of the quilt.

For simplicity's sake, let us suppose that we have either a square quilt top or a rectangular one. Make several photocopies of the sample quilts in Appendix B (page 92) to practice the exercises that follow. If you are particularly pleased with one or two of the "Block and Blank" exercises you have done, make several photocopies of these, too. (You will first need to transfer the entire design to your graph paper base from the tracing paper.)

The predictable approach is to center the block grouping within the perimeter. With a square grouping, there is another choice: whether to put the square parallel to the perimeter or at a 45 degree angle to it (on point).

Edges of block grouping parallel to perimeter.

Edges of block at a 45 degree angle to perimeter.

In order to reach for the unexpected, we must look for other positions for these block groupings. Instead of centering them, consider placing them purposely off-center.

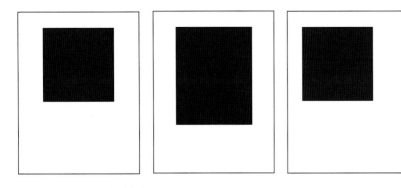

Alternative positions for block groupings

Place block grouping askew.

Another way to reach for the unexpected is to place the block grouping at some other angle in relation to the perimeter—placing the blocks "askew." When working with this option, remember to make corners of the block grouping, or major division lines of that grouping, coincide with the crossing of two graph paper lines of the background.

Create a perimeter for your quilt by placing a piece of tracing paper on a piece of graph paper. Using the graph paper lines as a guide, draw a rectangle, measuring 8" × 10". Take the photocopy of either the square or rectangular quilt from Appendix B (page 92), and place it between the tracing and graph paper according to one of the arrangements above (e.g. the square quilt on point, but not dead center in the quilt: or, the rectangular quilt, but at an askew angle within the perimeter). Now, using the block and blank approach to quilt design (change the angle, use bent lines, use interrupted lines, and so on), create an interesting setting for the quilt somewhere within the perimeter you have created.

The size of the perimeter can be determined by other factors: you may know the finished size of a bed quilt you are making, or you may count out a certain number of inches (squares on the graph paper) from the photocopied layout. The exercise in the paragraph above forces you to deal with a larger-than-normal border area!

Again, this may look like quite a piecing challenge at first—but the hints in Chapter Four (page 62) will put to rest all your fears about getting from design to templates to fabric. Like so many other facets of quilt-making, it will be a matter of taking one step at a time.

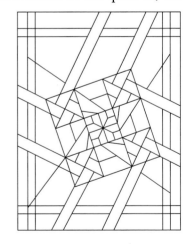

The setting for this square block grouping set askew with the quilt's perimeter was created by extending existing design lines and using interrupted lines. To keep the eye from running off the edge of the quilt, I created a border within a border with lines parallel to the quilt's edge and at different distances from it.

I THOUGHT I HAD
A GAME PLAN
38" × 38"
Rayna Gillman
West Orange, New Jersey,
1997.

This quilt grew on the design wall, not from a design on graph paper. Rayna used the "askew" approach within the quilt's perimeter most effectively. This quilt, with such a contemporary look, contains fabrics taken from a mutilated quilt made in the late 1800s! I hope the quiltmaker who made the original blocks (which are now living a new life in the nine-patches in Rayna's Quilt) is looking down with glee as she sees how the remnants of her string star quilt top have evolved!

SASHING STRIPS—VARIATIONS ON A THEME: ANOTHER AREA TO REACH FOR THE UNEXPECTED

The predictable approach to separating blocks from each other is to cut a strip of fabric that will, when sewn, separate the blocks by two inches in the final quilt. We have already experimented with innovative approaches to arranging blocks in the focus area of a quilt, and now we can apply the same "reach for the unexpected" approach to sashing strips.

Traditional sashing strips are placed between every block and every row of blocks, so consider grouping the blocks so that some blocks are not separated from each other at all. This would be most effective with appliqué blocks, pieced blocks with a central motif, or blocks which have a one inch wide border around them. Blocks both with and without borders are shown in the drawings on page 36.

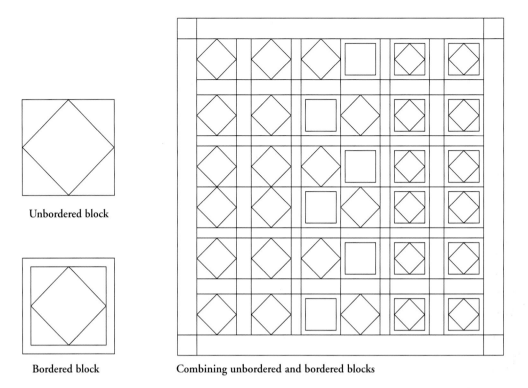

Unbordered block

Bordered block

Combining unbordered and bordered blocks

Whereas traditional sashing strips are all the same width throughout the quilt and made of one fabric, consider multiple fabrics, each of different widths.

Or put several fabrics together as one sashing strip as shown below. This would be a wonderful setting for four 18" appliqué blocks with either another appliqué or an elaborate pieced block in the center.

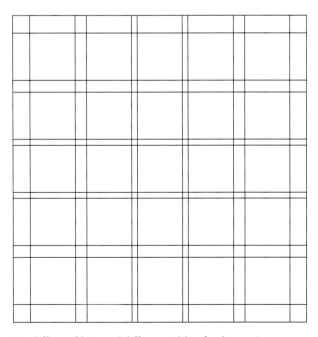

Use different fabrics and different widths of sashing strips.

Use several fabrics together for sashing strips.

Sashing strips are a good place to play with value. Instead of choosing just one fabric for the sashing strips, consider using a range of values. Go from very light in one area of the quilt to very dark in another. At the same time, consider a different value strategy for the setting squares; either keep all the setting squares the same value or make the movement of light to dark in the setting squares be the opposite of that in the sashing strips.

This approach would probably be more effective if all the blocks were the same pattern; or, if they were very similar in value and color, even though they might be all of a different pattern.

Once the ideas from this chapter begin to swirl in your head, you will find that innovative settings for quilt blocks will come to mind when you least expect them! So keep an idea book handy to jot down these fresh ideas, no matter how simple—or how silly— they seem at first glance! The danger is that you will try to incorporate too many ideas into the same quilt. Many quiltmakers naturally make designs that are too complex (the author included!) and then have to backtrack and simplify to arrive at a final pleasing design. Don't try to rush this process—enjoy the journey!

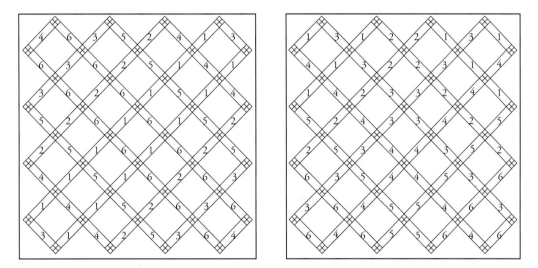

There are numerous ways to assign light-to-dark values to these sashing strip layouts; only two possibilities are shown here. Setting squares could be all light, all dark, or a checkerboarding of the two values that meet at the particular setting square. The #1 in the diagrams above represents the lightest value used, with the higher numbers representing successively darker values.

CHAPTER 3

Design Details:

TOOLS *of the* TRADE

In this chapter we will add some design elements to use to flesh out the layouts you may have come up with as a result of the exercises in Chapter Two.

BLOCK SEGMENTS

The first design element is called "block segments." Block segments are portions of patchwork blocks which are used as building blocks to create new designs in areas of the quilt outside the block itself. Block segments may be procured from blocks that already appear in the quilt, or they may come from other blocks that are not related to the quilt at all.

The best blocks to use for this exercise are simple in design, and usually four patch or nine patch blocks (five- and seven-patch blocks are often too complicated, and don't blend well with four- and nine-patch block segments). Blocks with a significant number of diagonal lines are better than those with mostly horizontal and vertical lines. If you have pieced block patterns in the set you are working with, start with those patterns before looking for other unrelated patchwork blocks.

To design with block segments, draft a number of your favorite blocks into one and one-half inch squares on a piece of eight-squares-per-inch graph paper. (Each block will be 12 little squares on a side). Make a whole column of each block. Include both four-patch and nine-patch patterns. Make at least five photocopies of this sheet, or make ten photocopies of Appendix A (page 91) to start with.

Cutting blocks apart goes more quickly if you use rotary cutting equipment rather than paper scissors, especially if you use the technique described on page 11. I always keep handy a second rotary cutter labeled "paper," in which I use the rotary blades that are no longer sharp enough to cut fabric. You will use paper scissors for other parts of this process.

Record the ideas you generate here in your Idea Book (page 7) by gluing down interesting combinations of block segments. You thus will be creating a "menu of motifs" from which you can later select innovative quilt setting designs. The more patchwork blocks you play with, the more extensive (and useful) this menu of motifs will become. To generate more ideas faster, do this exercise with your small quilting group, and share the results!

First, consider the ways these elements can be joined with each other.
• Right side up/upside down, alternated;
• Offset from each other by an amount for each block dependent on the specific line design in the block;
• On point—square segments on point, or rectangular ones laid at an angle;
• Overlapped, either transparent or opaque.

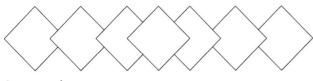

Opaque overlap

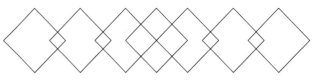

Transparent overlap

After you have played with like segments (quarter blocks with only other quarter blocks from the same quilt pattern) try combining various types of segments (such as quarter blocks with half blocks, etc.) from either the same or from several quilt block patterns.

In the following discussions, the basic cut is presented, followed by a number of ways you can put the separated pieces back together again, to create something other than the original block! In the sample rotations, there is a dot on the segment presented so you can tell when it has been turned upside down or rotated. You will probably discover additional rotations—make a note of each one using this "dot" notation so you can try it with other blocks. Paste the most interesting designs in your Idea Book.

THE BASIC CUTS

THE WHOLE BLOCK

Glue down a whole (uncut) block. After some of the cuts have been made, it will be hard to tell what the original block was without this whole block as a reference!

Note: Make the following cuts even though there are no seam lines where you are making the cut. For example, when you cut the block in half, you will probably be cutting on seam lines in part of the block but through the middle of some shapes in other parts of it (unless you are cutting a four patch block with a line down the middle of the block).

HALF BLOCK (RECTANGLES)

Cut the block down the middle, then see how many patterns you can make by rotating these two rectangles. Use them right side up, upside down, and sideways.

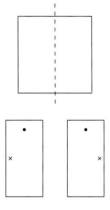

Yield: Two rectangles

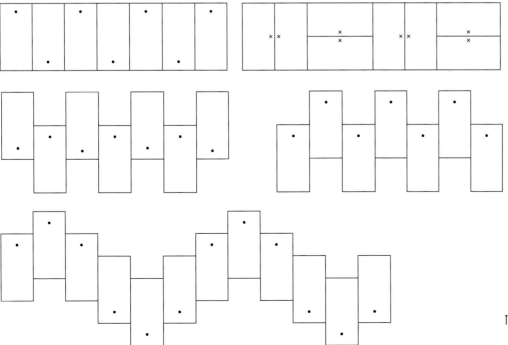

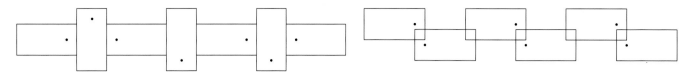

QUARTER BLOCK (SQUARES)

Cut the block in half down the middle then cut each of the rectangles in half crosswise.

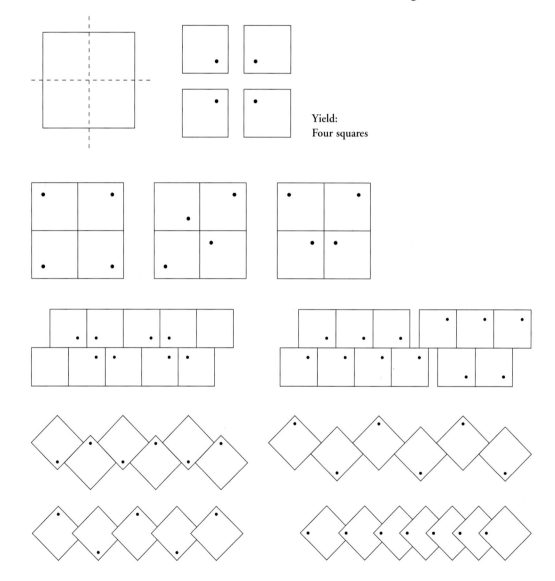

Yield:
Four squares

The Empty Spools at Asilomar quilts, (pages 19 and 24) all used a quarter of the Jewel Box block lined up very predictably as a border row. Note, however, that the same patchwork pattern looks very different depending on how the color is used within that block! Note also that by bringing some of the fabrics from the quilt's interior into the border (blue painted fabric in quilt III on page 24, and the butterscotch column fabric in quilt II on page 24), you can camouflage where the quilt stops and the border begins.

HALF BLOCK (CORNER TO CORNER)

Cut the block diagonally from corner to corner, then see how many patterns you can make by rotating these two triangles. Use them right side up, upside down, and sideways.

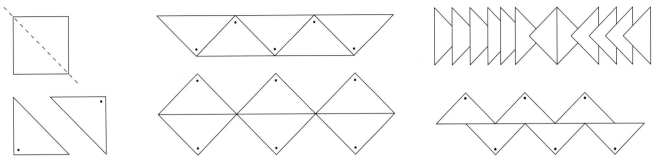

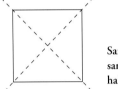

Yield: Two half-square triangles

QUARTER BLOCK (CORNER TO CORNER)

Cut the block in half diagonally from corner to corner, then cut each of the triangles in half diagonally.

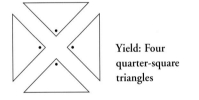

Same shape and same rotations as in half block.

Yield: Four quarter-square triangles

ALONG PATCH LINES

Patch lines are the divisions which make the block a nine-patch, a five-patch, and so on. Again, there may or may not be a seam line to mark this division in the block. With nine-patch blocks, cut along the patch lines in one direction only. If you cut along patch lines both ways, you are chopping up the block too finely. (Do not cut up the block so much that you are actually cutting out individual single shapes from the block.)

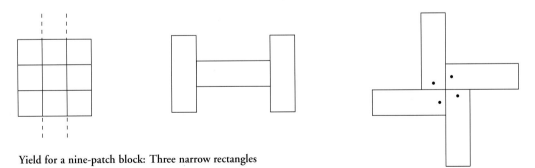

Yield for a nine-patch block: Three narrow rectangles

ALONG SEAM LINES

Now look at the line design of the block and see what segments would result if you cut along seam lines. Seam lines may go all the way across the block or go part way into the block, change direction, and come out on another side of the block.

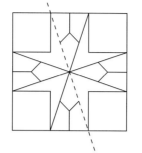

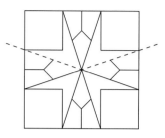

Seam lines may go all the way across the block, or they may change direction in the middle of the block, as in the example at right. Note that with this block you can create the illusion of a "swag" border.

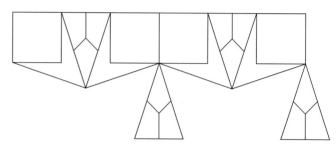

MEDORA ORANGE PEEL
62" × 62"
Margaret J. Miller

Woodinville, Washington, 1999. Machine quilted by Kathy Sandbach, Volcano, California. Collection of Delores Cameron, Miles City, Montana. Blocks made by quiltmakers attending Quilting in the Badlands 1998, a retreat in Medora, North Dakota. Note how effective variegated fabric was in this quilt; the burgundy-to-peach cloud fabric created a secondary cross in the background, and the blue fabric in the center enhances the medallion focus of the quilt. One of the twelve blocks seemed to lend itself to be a good corner block. The original block in the lower right corner of the quilt looked like this:

When I removed the shaded triangle in the drawing, and substituted another shape that went beyond the original block line and became a part of the interior of the quilt, this block took on quite a different role. Of course, then I had to make three more similar blocks for the other three corners!

LIGHTHOUSES
64" × 84"
Margaret J. Miller
Woodinville, Washington,
1998. Hand quilted by
members of various Atlanta
area quilt guilds at the
Atlanta History Center.
Collection of Anne C. Smith,
Gainesville, Georgia. Blocks
made by quilters attending
Retreat at Jekyll Island,
Georgia.

Notice that two-thirds of
the block entitled "Doris'
Delight" was used as the
basis for the border. In addition to using the block segments for this border, the
patch lines were moved so
that the nine-patch block
would become distorted,
giving it a refreshingly different look.

MANIPULATIONS OF THE BASIC CUTS

Now, using multiples of the block segments created previously, experiment with combinations of design motifs which might become an interesting part of the setting you are creating for your quilt blocks.

Combine different type segments: for instance, half-block right triangle with quarter-block squares or quarter-block triangles.

Add the element of value change to the idea of block segments. Think about using variegated fabrics in certain shapes. Or make your values in the border run light to dark in one shape, either along one side or from the middle to the corners.

Next, consider how these motifs can be related to the quilt:

Are you going to put these elements right at the edge of your quilt or farther away? Or both (near on side edges of the quilt and farther away from the top and bottom edges)?

Are you going to put them in groups, then relate the groups to the center area of the quilt by using Block and Blank techniques (pages 25–31)?

You can combine these segments with whole blocks and build all or part of your quilt like a jigsaw puzzle. The center of Mary Hales' *Starmaker Series IV* quilt (page 29) was created this way: the triangles north and south of the center block originally were one block in the friendship set. By undoing the corner-to-corner seam of that block, and making another block which expressed the same values and colors with my own fabrics, the setting for that center block was created.

In *Kerry's Hearts I* (page 14), I used the corner motifs of a block called Cross and Crown. This is part of a five-patch block pattern, but I used it as though it were a quarter block. I placed these quarter blocks where the heart blocks were offset in order to soften the harsh edges of the ring of blocks, a technique similar to tucking baby's breath into a bouquet of flowers to soften the overall effect of the bouquet.

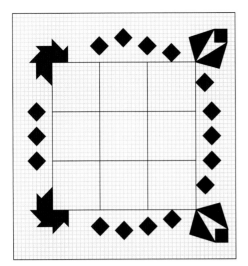

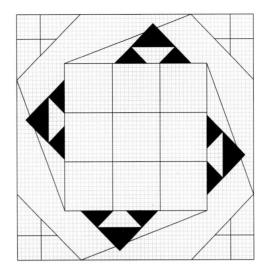

This illustration depicts the same arrangement of block segments top and bottom, but different arrangements of segments along the side edges. Notice the different corner treatments as well. The next step in the designing process is to add design lines that will relate these block segments to the body of the quilt.

Block segments used in each grouping—one half-block triangle and two quarter-block triangles

Delores Cameron's quilt *Medora Orange Peel* (page 42) was one of four quilts made from the blocks brought to a North Dakota quilter's retreat in 1998. In addition to taking a corner triangle off one block to use as a corner turning, as previously discussed, I disassembled two more of the 12 blocks Delores won, in order to get all the blocks into a cohesive setting. The four Attic Window blocks off the corners of the center block were originally in a single quilt block, separated by half-inch wide black strips of fabric. Also, the four five-strip blocks used as "north, south, east, and west" links to the bordered blocks were also originally one rail-fence type block. By disassembling these two blocks, I created not only a reasonable number of blocks to work with, but also additional design elements of a different size than the majority of the blocks in the set.

See Linda Gunby's quilt *Horsin' Around with the Sisters* (page 30) for another example of various smaller units being used to create a mosaic-like whole. The four flying geese units were originally a Dutchman's Puzzle block. The trail of squares is really a series of four patches. Finally, the tiny nine-patch squares seemed entirely unrelated to the 12-inch squares in this set, but create a fine design detail in the final quilt.

Another quilt which shows innovative use of block segments is Connie Tiegel's quilt *Sisterhood Special—and a Side of Stars* on page 46. The chain of squares reaching out to the border builds on the pattern begun within four of the original blocks in the set.

Notice how continuing this chain of dark squares with more four-patches on point through the star block inner border camouflages somewhat where the quilt stops and the border begins. The flower-like image that resulted when the four patches meet the star border—was yet another unexpected surprise in the design process!

SISTERHOOD SPECIAL—AND A SIDE OF STARS

61" × 61"

Margaret J. Miller

Woodinville, Washington, 1998. Collection of Connie L. Tiegel, Atherton, California. Blocks made by six-member friendship group called Sisterhood of the Purple, which has kept a round-robin letter circulating among its members since its inception in 1995.

Notice also the shapes made of striped fabrics next to the center group of nine blocks on point. This is a good example of how important changing the angle can be in quilt design. If those shapes were not there, the quilt design would be much more rigid; since none of the three lines creating those shapes are at a 45 degree angle to the edges of the quilt, they soften the look of the quilt considerably. The orange-and-blue striped inner border was the last design element added. The white space between the star border and the central motif was too vast; the central design was lost in the middle of the quilt before that last inner border was added.

Diagonal lines form a ribbon behind the block.

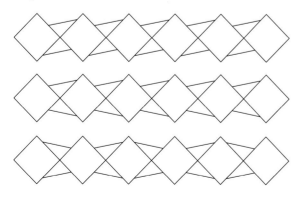

Alternative ways to link star blocks on point

The little nine-patch star in the border of this quilt is fun to work with. In Connie's quilt, what makes the stars "dance" around the quilt are the diagonal lines that seem to form a ribbon behind them. Note the design points that were used to create this ribbon— this is another example of the principle of the interrupted line.

The slightly larger blocks where this ribbon of stars "rounds the corners" also illustrate a good change in scale of design. Even though the motif is a pinwheel and not a star, there is still a "star-like feeling" to these larger blocks.

At left are some other ways to link star blocks (or other small motifs) on point.

REPEAT DESIGN ELEMENTS

Some design elements that are mainstays in patchwork lend themselves to innovative block settings. Flying-geese triangles, pinwheels and diamonds made from half-square triangles, Rail Fence blocks, small-scale four patches, and nine patches are just a few of these. There are numerous simple designs, a few of which appear below, that lend themselves to fleshing out overall quilt block layouts. You may have other favorites of your own.

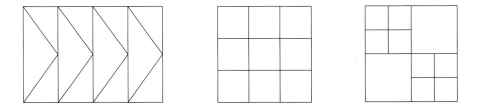

Simple design elements

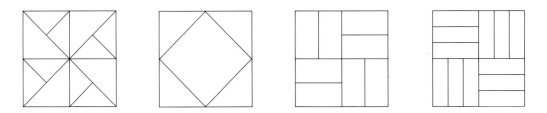

There are two main ways to reach for the unexpected when using a repeat design. One is to change something about that repeat design as it moves across the quilt. That "something" could be bold (color, scale of print) or subtle (moving value from light to dark). You can also take that repeat design, and make it follow a surprising pathway (see Linda Gunby's quilt, page 30). Or, make a row of that element asymmetrical (ex. Pinwheel in Nancy Thorne's *Don't Fence Me In*, page 52) rather than symmetrical. Or, make it move in an unexpected pathway, like an undulating line rather than a straight, rigid one for flying geese (see drawing on page 51).

"Making things change" when you are using a regular repeat design not only makes the quilt more interesting to look at, it's more interesting to piece as well. In the sections that follow, we'll take a closer look at the specific elements: Flying Geese, Rail Fence, and four patches and nine patches.

FLYING GEESE

The Flying Geese pattern is so versatile because it is a directional element and rectangular in shape, and hence it is symmetrical two ways, not four. Therefore there are many ways you can vary its movement in the quilt: you can change its direction, its relative position in a path of geese, the length of the individual triangle at its base, and its height. Since it is a repeat element, you can also change the fabric in the line of geese here and there for an additional sparkle.

INDIAN SUMMER

90" × 90"

Maggie Ball

Bainbridge Island, Washington, 1998.
Maggie's Christmas present one year was having this quilt machine quilted by Wanda Rains, Bainbridge Island, Washington. Maggie sold this quilt to a gentleman who donated it in honor of his late wife to a fund-raising auction to benefit Bainbridge Island Arts and Crafts. The quilt is now in the collection of Tuck and Jax Donnelly of Bainbridge Island, Washington, the winners of that auction.

One way to use flying geese is to fill a shape in the quilt with them. Maggie Ball used flying geese in a very dignified manner, but note how her use of color adds a touch of whimsy. The red geese "round the bend" at the end of the diagonals, keeping the eye from going off the corner of her quilt. Also, Maggie's use of flying geese in a medium size is such a nice complement to the triangles in the interior blocks and to the sawtooth edge on the inner gold-colored medallion.

BUILDING COMMUNITY I

73" × 73"

Louise Dressen

Kirkland, Washington, 1997.
Quilted by the members of the Holy Spirit Lutheran Church of Kirkland, Washington. Collection of Christine Wornack, Bellevue, Washington. This and *Building Community II* (page 27) were made to raise funds among several local Lutheran church communities for two Habitat for Humanity projects; the residents of the new homes now own the quilts.

Louise filled a more irregular shape with flying geese. Note how much more dimension is added to the quilt by the fact that Louise graded values from light to dark in each pathway of flying geese triangles.

One quilt in which I have used flying geese extensively is in my quilt *Sunbonnet Sue Goes Bowling*, (page 13), the blocks of which were made by a small quilt group in my area who call themselves "Monday Night Bowling League" instead of some "patchworky" title!

Another way to use flying geese effectively is to make an undulating row of them; this makes a stronger border than if all the triangles were the same size and lined up at the same level.

Geese are useful for making a medallion around a single block or a group of blocks.

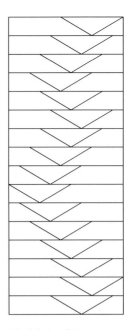

Undulating flying geese

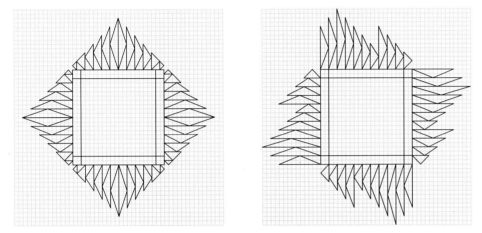

Flying geese in different heights

Whenever you use a repeat pattern such as flying geese, look for ways to introduce different colors or values in any grouping of geese, to add interest. You may add a brighter color every now and then, or perhaps move carefully from light to dark to light again in certain areas of the quilt.

RAIL FENCE

The strip-pieced Rail Fence pattern is very versatile for creating background settings for traditional patchwork blocks. Rail Fence blocks can be made of any number of strips from two to five. Most commonly, they are two- or three-strip blocks. The Rail Fence blocks can be rotated to create different patterns: diagonal zigzags, diamonds, stars (or crosses), and pinwheels, to name a few.

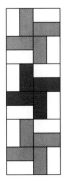
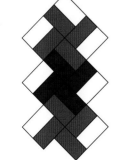

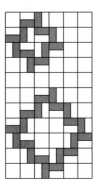

Rail Fence blocks rotated to create different patterns

The idea for considering rail fence in this way came from making Cathie Hoover's *Special Messages* quilt (page 23). Two of the blocks contributed for that quilt were rail fence designs: one a zigzag, the other pinwheels (see upper right and lower right inner corners of that quilt). Notice how the zigzags from those inner corners were continued into the next border—they

interrupt the "X's and O's" (kisses and hugs) at the center of each side. This is another example of camouflaging where the quilt stops and a given border begins.

Another possibility would be to combine two- and three-strip Rail Fence blocks in the same quilt background. Yet another idea is to let the motif transform from one shape to another—let the zigzags yield to a row of pinwheels, then a row of ribbon weave, and so on.

DON'T FENCE ME IN
69" × 69"
Margaret J. Miller
Woodinville, Washington, 1999. Machine quilted by Kathy Sandbach, Volcano, California. Collection of Nancy J. Thorne, Merlin, Oregon. One of four quilts from blocks made by quilt-makers attending the Quilting in the Badlands 1998 retreat in Medora, North Dakota.

The three-strip Rail Fence blocks have been rotated to form a zigzag pattern. That zigzag, if centered in the quilt, could have formed a diamond behind the arrangement of offset quilt blocks. But instead, by putting it off-center and continuing the zigzag into the border, it forms a pinwheel behind the blocks.

STARS OVER MEDORA
69" × 69"
Margaret J. Miller
Woodinville, Washington,
1999. Machine quilted by
Kathy Sandbach, Volcano,
California. Collection of Dixie
A. Whitmer, Bloomfield,
Montana. Dixie won these
blocks at the Quilting in the
Badlands 1998 retreat in
Medora, North Dakota.
The idea for this quilt woke
me out of a sound sleep
one night as the book deadline approached. This quilt
and *Don't Fence Me In*
(page 52) are the result of
that sleepless night!

A two-strip Rail Fence Block
was used in *Stars Over
Medora*. This quilt was complicated in that each star
motif involved five different
fabrics; to get the stars to
interlock, the quiltmaker has
to pay close attention to the
way this jigsaw puzzle goes
together! I first saw this pattern was one of the blocks by
Christine Porter of Bristol,
England made for Cathie
Hoover's *Special Messages*
quilt (page 23). It lends itself
very well, in a low contrast
version, to be a background
for sampler blocks.

The important element in this quilt is not so much the star motif itself but the manip-
ulation of contrast (which makes the stars seem to sparkle against the background of more
stars) and the movement of value from light in the center to dark at the outer edges. By
keeping the center of the quilt lighter in value, the focus stays on the eight blocks. The
stars made from Rail Fence blocks do not become distracting; rather, they form the textured backdrop they were meant to be.

FOUR PATCHES AND NINE PATCHES

We have already alluded to using four patches as a way of leading the eye around the
quilt, but they can also be used as design elements. (See Linda Gunby's and Connie
Tiegel's quilts, pages 30 and 46.) Aligning a trail of dark squares by putting four- or nine-
patch blocks point-to-point can be a very effective method for leading the eye around a
quilt or out of a given block to camouflage where it stops and its background begins.
With nine-patch blocks, you can have a bold trail of diamonds and a subtle secondary
trail on either side.

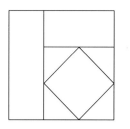

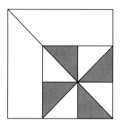

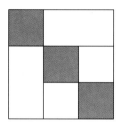

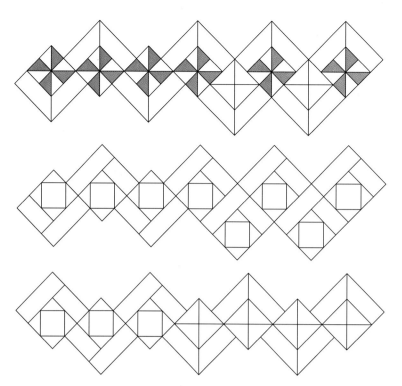

Offset the blocks to create a link

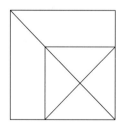

Add strips to two adjacent sides of the block.

ASYMMETRY: NEW LIFE FOR REPEAT DESIGN ELEMENTS

You can take a very simple repeat design element, add to it, then offset it so it becomes an asymmetrical use of a symmetrical element. For example, in Virginia Avery's sisterhood quilt (page 20) note that the border is basically a row of four-patch blocks alternated with pinwheels made up of half-square triangles, both of which are fairly unrelated in color. Adding strips to two adjacent sides of these little blocks gives them a whole new life by changing them from four-patch to nine-patch patterns.

They can be lined up in a number of ways, but by offsetting them, you create a link that isn't obvious at first glance in the individual blocks.

BORDER WITHIN A BORDER

Since we are defining "border" as an area of the quilt in which the quilt can come to a gradual visual close, we have choices as to where that area can begin. In many quilts in this book, there is a "border within the border," a design element that announces that the visual finish of the quilt is near. A good example is in Nancy Thorne's *Don't Fence Me In* (page 52). Without the striped columns, the diagonals formed by the Rail Fence blocks would have led the eye right off the edge of the quilt, taking the focus away from the patchwork blocks.

Other quilts which have this feature include those shown on pages 10, 13, 17, and 18.

FABRIC CHOICES

My motto is: "Never use two fabrics when you can use twenty!" My favorites are prints rather than solids, as they are easier to blend with each other. I also like to use striped fabrics for added punch and design possibilities in a given design. In Mary Hales's *Starmaker Series II*, I used sections of a striped fabric to accentuate the three-dimensional nature of the folded ribbon border.

You can see the uncut striped fabric in the first borders around each block. Since the stripe had both teal and peach sections, it was easy to use it to portray different sides of the same ribbon.

In Nancy Thorne's *Don't Fence Me In* (page 52), note how stripes create a strong "border within the border" when set at an angle within that border shape. Stripes can create texture in a background that would otherwise be bland, and can move the eye around a quilt by filling certain shapes (see Connie Tiegel's sisterhood quilt, page 46).

In every quilt, try to go "up to the lights" and "down to the darks" in the values you incorporate into the setting for your quilt blocks. If you want your blocks to blend into the background as though they were part of a watercolor painting, use a narrower range of value and not much contrast between the blocks and the background. If you want the blocks to be the focus of the surface, use high contrast between the blocks and their background, and use as wide a range of value from light light to dark dark as possible.

When trying to move from light to dark across the surface of the quilt, put a few of your lightest pieces and a few of your darkest pieces in place on the design wall. These could be the actual shapes cut with templates or pieces of the lightest and darkest fabrics you have chosen. Pin them to the wall in the general vicinity of where you know your lightest and darkest areas will be. This will help you see what fabric choices to make in the middle.

Most importantly, don't let yourself stop and agonize during the process of cutting out the quilt. Start with what you are sure of (or at least what you have a strong idea about) and let the rest of the quilt emerge. If you find yourself agonizing, take a break—take a walk or have a cup of tea or vacuum a room or straighten a shelf—and come back at a later time, even if it is only 10 minutes later!

STARMAKER SERIES II
65" × 30"
Margaret J. Miller
Woodinville, Washington, 1998. Machine quilted by Heather Tewell, Anacortes, Washington. Collection of Mary E. Hales, Mount Vernon, Washington.

The best thing that can happen to you is that you run out of a given fabric, for you will have to substitute another which "sings the same song." I hardly ever buy more than one yard of fabric at a time, so I am constantly making substitutions. Look at the border of Connie Tiegel's sisterhood quilt (page 46); the only reason there are two very different types of stripes is that I didn't have enough of either one to complete that border!

Notice how the eye is led around your quilt by your placement of value. Does the quilt have light colors in the center and gradually get darker at the edges? You need not edge with dark fabrics to bring the quilt to a visual close. The background in Nancy Thorne's border blocks go from light in the center to dark to light again at the edge of the quilt (page 52).

Another way of moving the eye around the quilt is by manipulating value in a certain shape or group of shapes. In the *Quilting by the Lake Scholarship Quilt* (page 57) the progressive values in the triangles behind the outermost blocks helps give movement to the block setting and bring light to an otherwise fairly dark set of blocks.

MANET'S ROBIN
65" × 65"
Final border by Margaret J. Miller Woodinville, Washington, 1991. Machine quilted by Kathy Sandbach, Volcano, California. Collection of Margaret Ann Liston, Seattle, Washington.

When planning fabric and color placement, spread a given fabric or color evenly across the quilt surface. *Manet's Robin* is a round robin quilt project for which I was to create the final border, based on "points." The quilt was beautiful and seemed finished when it arrived. It ended at the edge of the blue "celestial" print and was already quite large. Notice that the final border, begun by absent-mindedly sewing strips left over from a previous border, is successful because the peach color was reintroduced. Before my border, the peach color appeared in the center only. It is as though I completed the color sentence someone else had started.

QUILTING BY THE LAKE SCHOLARSHIP QUILT
58" × 58"

Margaret J. Miller

Woodinville, Washington, 1999.

Collection of Rebecca LaBarr, Oneonta, New York. The blocks for this quilt were won at Quilting by the Lake in Morrisville, New York, by Janet Inscoe of Douglasville, Georgia. Janet challenged me to put this eclectic group of blocks into a quilt. I did, and the quilt was raffled off in 1999 to support the scholarship fund for Quilting by the Lake, which enables quiltmakers to attend this conference when they would otherwise be unable to do so.

MARION'S FEATHERED FRIENDS
64" × 64"

Margaret J. Miller

Woodinville, Washington, 1999.

Machine quilted by Kathy Sandbach, Volcano, California. Blocks made by friends of Marion Shelton Harlan.

This sampler quilt is unusual because it is a very large setting for only nine sampler blocks. As complex as it looks, its design is very simple (see line drawing on page 69). I use more fabrics, rather than fewer, in any given quilt so that the more the viewer looks at these quilts, the more he or she sees there. The theme block "He Will Cover You with His Feathers" seemed to suggest birds in the trees to me, hence all the greens in the quilt.

The diamond structure behind the blocks is not one green fabric, but two. Also note the use of the thin rust-to-gold variegated fabric, which is the "golden lining" of that diamond structure as well as of the outermost border. In the center, using multiple blue fabrics strip-pieced together rather than a single blue one created shapes that seem to fan out from the center block.

OFFSETTING BLOCKS AND OTHER ELEMENTS TO CREATE MOVEMENT

Whenever possible during the design process, I look for ways to shake up the placement of a group of blocks. Where they are normally placed evenly, I offset them; where they are expected to be dead center, I purposely place them off center. Where they are normally in a rigid ring, I try to make them spin in a number of ways. These attempts do not always last until the final making of the quilt, but they are definitely part of every design process. With every quilt, I am trying to reach for the unexpected in any way I can, as long as it doesn't make the total picture bizarre or hard to understand.

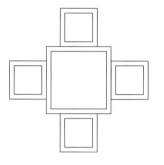

Traditional layout

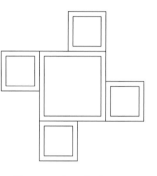

Unexpected—spinning

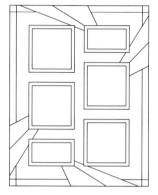

Large blocks arranged in columns and offset by a half a block, allow creation of half blocks on top right and lower left. Angled lines interrupt the borders and create movement.

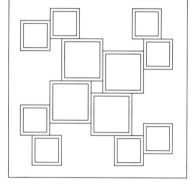

Large blocks offset to appear to spin around center space; smaller blocks offset to accentuate graceful spinning effect.

BUTTERFLY DÉJÀ VU
45" × 45"
Annette L. Clark
Chesapeake, Virginia, 1999.

This was the result of a monthly challenge from a local quilt shop in which participants receive a kit of fabric and a "bare bones" guideline. This challenge started with scraps of black, various pieces of the Alexander Henry line of butterfly and peacock prints, and instructions to use squares and half-square triangles.

Annette allowed the action to escape into her "border within a border," but note how she completed some quilt blocks and not others in that black inner area. This "escaping" effect was accentuated by the butterflies sprinkled throughout.

The center of this quilt was made in a workshop taught by Linda Dixon in Boise, based on the Square Dance technique developed by Martha Thompson of Lakewood, Colorado (see bibliography). Later, Cathie revised the workshop instructions to create the stars in varying sizes, and placed them innovatively in the border area.

Cathie took a "let the motifs escape" approach by changing the scale and placement of the theme motif in the border area. This quilt features a very regular star pattern in the body of the quilt; by varying the technique to create larger and smaller versions of the same star, she created a wonderful setting for this quilt, one which makes me want to make a wish every time I look at it!

LETTING THE ACTION ESCAPE

One effective way to camouflage where the quilt stops and the border begins is to let the action of the center of the quilt escape into the border in unexpected ways.

The mechanism by which you let the action of the quilt escape need not be a complicated design related to the quilt. I use the following border design on occasion; it can be used as a border for any quilt. If you have a borderless quilt top you made years ago and you can't buy more of the fabrics in the center of the quilt, this would be a good way for you to finish off such a project.

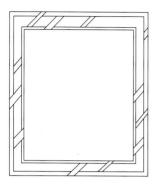

Let action escape into border by using diagonal shafts of light and/or color that weave over and under the border.

The diagonal strips are devices with which you can let the color from the quilt "shoot out" of the center for interest. These strips are not so strong that they lead the eye right off the edge of the quilt, since some are high contrast and others are lower contrast to the three main border fabrics. This border is best created by drawing it to scale and working with templates as described on pages 63–66. It does involve partial piecing, but the visual effect is worth spending a little time on its assembly.

Another way to use "action motifs" is exemplified by Mary Hales's *Thanks for the Good Times* quilt.

This same camouflaging effect can be created by using various width sashing strips in certain areas of the quilt (but not separating every block from its neighbor) as shown on page 36. Together they become a gridwork or trellis through which you are looking at something mysterious—a garden of quilt blocks, the quilt itself!

THANKS FOR THE
GOOD TIMES
60" × 60"
Margaret J. Miller
Woodinville, Washington,
1998. Collection of Mary E.
Hales, Mount Vernon,
Washington.

This quilt is comprised of very awkward elements: very long signature panels, combined with small three-inch pieced star blocks made by numerous well-wishers. The panels could not be cut into any smaller shapes, or someone's message would be cut in half. The solution to such an awkward design was to appliqué stars cascading across the quilt corner to corner, with a few escaping out into the border in unexpected places. It now looks like you are looking at the quilt through a galaxy of stars!

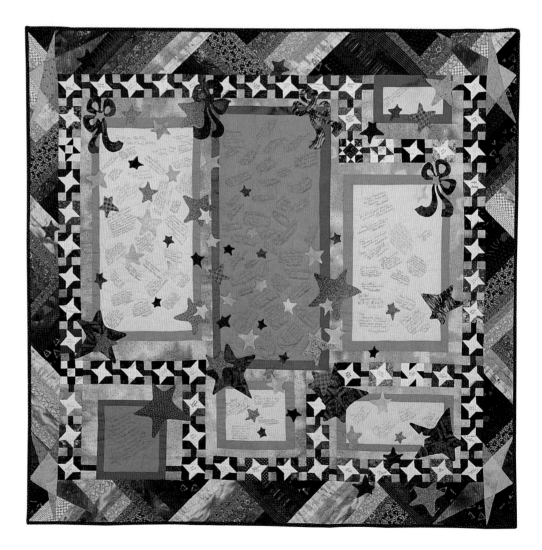

A CHECKLIST

In this chapter, I have presented a number of mechanisms you can use to breathe new design life into the setting for sampler blocks. It is more likely that you will get too complicated in your design, rather than not complicated enough. The trick is to stop yourself before you overdo it by getting too many visual tricks into one quilt surface!

As you are working out your scale drawing on graph paper, every so often pin it up on your design wall and stand back to look at it with a critical eye. Once in a while turn it upside down to the way you have been working with it to see if that leads to new design insights! Once you have settled on the design on graph paper, as you cut the shapes for the quilt and place them on the design wall, use your reducing glass often to stand back and look at your design again. Think about the following questions as you gaze at your design on the wall:

- Does the design flow well? Is the design of the setting so complicated that it overwhelms the blocks?
- Is there a balance between pieced and unpieced areas? Sometimes I discover after all the shapes are cut and on the design wall that I need to go back in and strip piece some of them, or add a design line or two within a given shape. This helps blend value a little better, or puts visual texture where the quilt looks "bare" because a single shape is too large.
- How does the contrast look? Have you used high contrast in the areas where you want to draw the most attention?
- Does your quilt have a resting place for the eyes?
- Is there a movement of light to dark in your quilt? Have you used an appropriately wide range of values in the setting for your blocks?
- Have you used enough different fabrics in your quilt? Look at all the areas where you have used the same fabric. Could you express the same color and value using two or even four similar fabrics?
- Are there little surprises built in? Will there be more to see in your quilt the longer the viewer looks at it?
- Most importantly, don't be afraid to go back and alter your graph paper design at any time during the process. It's never too late to change the design, until (perhaps) the point at which the quilting begins!

CHAPTER 4

The Piecing Process:

FROM PAPER DESIGN *to* REAL QUILTS

Making and using templates for the piecing process has gotten a bad reputation over the years. With the advent of the rotary cutter and accurate Plexiglas cutting guides, the process of cutting out a quilt has sped up considerably. Some people think that using templates therefore is old-fashioned and that it adds more steps to the process. But for some designs, templates are indispensable and don't add that much time to the process.

The template process I use I have gleaned over the years and modified to my own purposes. Debbie Caffrey of Anchorage, Alaska, first introduced me to using graph paper alone. Using freezer paper templates was one of the "Eureka!" experiences I had in Designing From Nature class with Ruth McDowell. I use both of these methods in the creation of my smashing samplers.

The templates are inexpensive, easy to store and retrieve during the piecing process, and disposable. Also, if you misplace a template, it is easy to create a duplicate (especially if you use the freezer paper technique).

SUPPLIES

- **Graph paper:** I use 17" × 22" pads of either eight-squares-per-inch or four-squares-per-inch graph paper for making templates. Take all graph paper for a given project from the same tablet of graph paper and use the same side of all the sheets in the tablet. For scale drawings, I use eight-squares-per-inch pads, in either 8¹/₂" × 11" or 11" × 17" tablets.

- **Pencils, pencil sharpener, eraser, paper scissors**

- **Rulers for drafting:** Use long flat ones (not Plexiglas® straightedges, which cast shadows on the paper, interfering with accuracy). Use a yardstick for drawing long lines.

- **Rubber Cement:** For joining sheets of graph paper.

- **Temporary adhesive:** This is for temporarily adhering graph paper templates to fabric. Double stick tape with some of its "stickiness" removed also serves this purpose.

- **Large flat space to create full-size drawing:** If you don't have a large dining room table and must work on the floor, use gardeners' kneelers or knee pads to protect your knees.

- **Supplies for cutting out templates:** Use a large rotary mat, rotary cutter with blades too dull to cut fabric, and both long and short Plexiglas straightedges. For adding accurate quarter-inch seam allowances, I prefer the rulers with yellow lines every inch and a grid of black lines every eighth inch.

- **Three-ring binder for templates:** To store paper templates until all the shapes have been cut, I three-hole punch colored typing paper and put it in a binder. Since the templates have temporary adhesive on them they stick to the paper, are more obvious, and easy to retrieve.

- **Supplies for cutting out fabric shapes:** You will need pencils for marking fabric: a #2 lead pencil, a silver pencil, and a red pencil; a pencil sharpener; a rotary mat and Plexiglas straightedges as above; a rotary cutter with blade sharp enough to cut fabric; and large Plexiglas squares. I use 6", 12", and 17" Plexiglas squares.

CREATING THE SCALE DRAWING

If you have been designing using tissue paper overlays over graph paper and colored-paper blanks glued in place, it is important to make yourself a good, accurate drawing of your scale design. Step one, therefore, is to transfer your design from tracing paper overlays to a piece of eight-squares-per-inch graph paper.

Next, study your design to see if you need to add any seam lines to facilitate the piecing process. Remember that any time a point comes out into an open area, you must add a seam line to be able to piece this shape into place. In the diagram below, the dotted lines are the lines that had to be added to make piecing of this quilt possible.

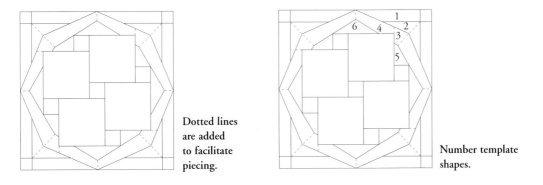

Dotted lines are added to facilitate piecing.

Number template shapes.

Number each of the different kinds of templates you need to create your quilt. If a template appears more than once in the quilt, only one shape needs to be numbered. This number system, which you will also mark on your full-size templates, will make it easier to retrieve your templates quickly during the fabric cutting process.

Do this numbering in an orderly fashion: for example if you have a quilt that has an inner ribbon border, number all the border shapes first, then the ribbon shapes, then the interior.

CREATING FULL-SIZE TEMPLATES

Study your design to determine how much of it you actually have to draw full size. In the drawing above, the numbered templates are the only ones that need to be drawn; since all four corners are identical, the same set of templates can be used to create all of them.

You will probably need to join large sheets of graph paper to be able to draw some parts of the quilt full size. In order to join two pieces of graph paper, first cut off two corners of the sheet you are adding to the base sheet. This allows you to see the horizontal and vertical lines at the same time as you are trying to align the graph paper lines.

Always use rubber cement to join graph paper sheets, as this is the only adhesive that doesn't bubble or shrink the graph paper.

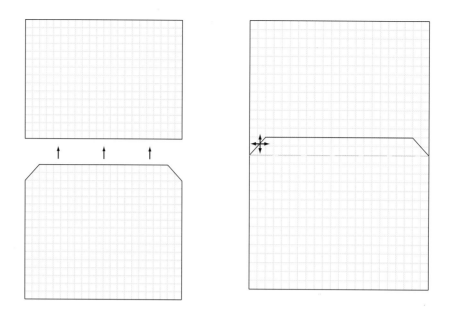

Cut off two corners of the sheet you are adding to the base sheet.

If you need to join more pieces of graph paper, always join enough pieces to adhere along a single straight edge: you never want to put yourself in the position of having to align graph paper lines on adjacent sides of a piece of graph paper!

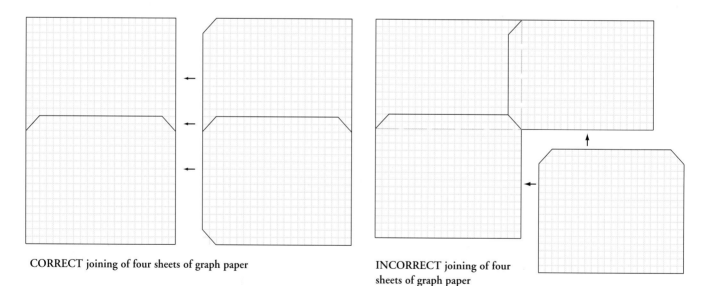

CORRECT joining of four sheets of graph paper

INCORRECT joining of four sheets of graph paper

Draw your quilt design full size. Remember that one little square on the graph paper represents one square inch full size. Now you see the importance of placing every design point at the intersection of two graph paper lines! To draw any angle, all you need to do is count inches which correspond to the little squares on your scale drawing. Once you find the beginning and ending design points of any line at an unusual angle, all you have to do is connect the dots!

USING THE GRAPH PAPER TEMPLATES

Once the design is drawn full size, number the templates exactly as they are numbered on the scale drawing. I add a grain line arrow parallel to the outside edges of the quilt; I always try to cut these edges on the lengthwise grain of the fabric. For greater accuracy, cut out templates using rotary cutting equipment, not scissors.

If there are square and rectangular shapes in your design, do not bother making a paper template for these. Use your Plexiglas squares to rotary cut these shapes from fabric. Be sure to add the quarter-inch seam allowance; if you have a shape that is 3" × 4" finished, cut out a fabric rectangle that measures 3¹/₂" × 4¹/₂".

Do not cut out all the paper templates at once. Cut them *only as you need them*. When cutting out templates, cut beyond the actual shape you are cutting out. Cut as long a line as the design permits. This way, every place a shape hits this line, the design points stay aligned, rather than jumping to either side of it.

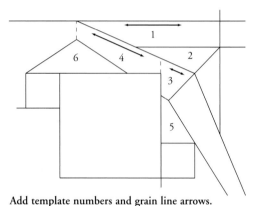

Add template numbers and grain line arrows.

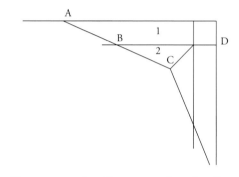

To cut out template #1, rotary cut from A to C, not merely from A to B. Then templates #1 and #2 will align perfectly, once the B-D side has been cut.

Take the paper template to the fabric and put a strip of temporary adhesive on the back side of the template. Adhere it to the right side of the fabric, lining up one edge of the template on the straight grain of the fabric. Your design will determine which edge to align; whenever you have a bias edge, try to sew a straight grain edge to it.

Using your Plexiglas straightedge with the eighth-inch grid lines on it, align the cut edge of the paper template with the ¹/₄" line on the ruler. Cut. Do this on all sides of the template.

When you have a shape with an elongated point such as a triangle, place the quarter-inch cross-hairs on the point of the paper triangle, and place the quarter-inch line of the ruler on one of the paper edges leading to that point. Trim.

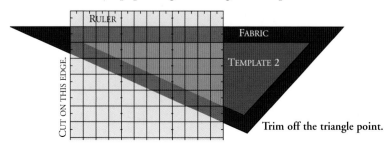

Trim off the triangle point.

If you have several identical shapes in the quilt, you can stack multiple fabrics (all right side up) and cut them all at the same time. If you have mirror image shapes in the quilt, stack the fabrics with half of the fabrics right side up and half with wrong sides up. I never try to cut more than four layers at a time, and always keep very sharp blades in my rotary cutter to ensure accuracy for this process. Take the paper template off the fabric and place the fabric shape in position on your design wall. Store the paper template in your three-ring binder of colored papers and go on to the next shape you need.

SEWING THE QUILT TOGETHER

The secret of success in this system is trying to be as careful and accurate as you can at all stages of the process—*do not rush!*

Obviously you must sew the same seam allowance that you added to your paper templates. So before you sew the first two shapes together, perform this test. While you are cutting out the shapes, take one fabric shape to the sewing machine *before you remove the paper template* from it. Place the paper and fabric under the presser foot of the sewing machine and lower the needle so that it touches the edge of the paper template. Notice where the edge of the cut fabric is—the edge of the fabric is what you should use as your quarter-inch seam guide on the sewing machine. This may or may not be what you currently use as your seam guide.

You will probably be cutting fabrics one template at a time at first. But as your quilt begins to take shape on the design wall, you may find areas of the quilt in which you can sew two fabrics together first, then cut a double template from these fabrics already sewn together. This not only increases the accuracy of your piecing, it saves a lot of time. This is especially useful if you have very small shapes to piece.

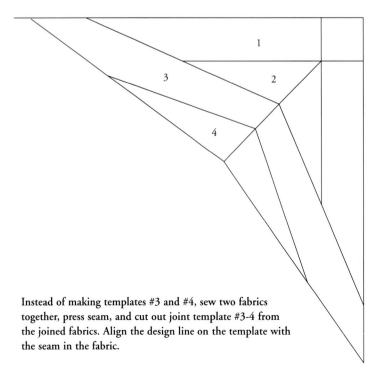

Instead of making templates #3 and #4, sew two fabrics together, press seam, and cut out joint template #3-4 from the joined fabrics. Align the design line on the template with the seam in the fabric.

THE FREEZER PAPER TECHNIQUE: VARIATION ON A THEME

Use the freezer paper technique if your quilt has many tiny or awkwardly-shaped pieces.

This technique is the same as the graph paper technique in its earliest phases—you still draw full size as much of your scale drawing as you need to piece the quilt. Number the full-size templates to correspond with your scale drawing.

Trace the templates onto freezer paper shiny side up using a Sharpie® felt pen. Transfer template numbers and markings to the non-shiny side of the freezer paper.

Cut out freezer paper shapes only as needed. Cut out with rotary cutting equipment, as previously mentioned.

To transfer to fabric: adhere freezer paper shiny side down on the wrong side of the fabric. Using a ruler with an eighth-inch grid, cut out fabric a quarter inch away from the edge of the freezer paper. Trim elongated points as with graph paper. Optional: trace around freezer paper shape with pencil, or leave freezer paper adhered to fabric. The edges of the freezer paper can be used as a sewing guide.

Freezer paper templates can be removed from the fabric and adhered to other fabrics multiple times. As with the graph paper templates, you can put a "joint" freezer paper template (two templates cut as one) on the back of two fabrics already sewn together.

SEWING TECHNIQUES

It doesn't matter where you start piecing your quilt; the quilt will never let you get ahead of yourself. Sometimes, however, you must do what is known as partial piecing. This means that there are some seams you can't sew until you partially join two other pieces. Then you can sew the joined shapes (which are actually sewn together at only one end of the seam), to the longer edge.

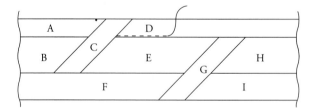

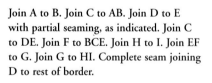

Join A to B. Join C to AB. Join D to E with partial seaming, as indicated. Join C to DE. Join F to BCE. Join H to I. Join EF to G. Join G to HI. Complete seam joining D to rest of border.

Since you are now free to use numerous angles to create an interesting design, you will not automatically be sewing raw edge to raw edge on every seam. Whenever three or more seams come together, you will be sewing only from the beginning of the seam, leaving the seam allowances free. Some shapes you will set in as you do with the traditional Y-seam construction.

The most important aspects of sewing are to take your time and avoid rushing! Accuracy is a skill that is acquired; the more you work at it, the better you get. The sewing process is exciting in that your design really begins to "crisp up" as you begin to join the pieces; the jigsaw puzzle finally comes together into its magnificent whole!

CHAPTER 5

PROJECTS *for* YOU

In this chapter, line drawings are presented for many of the quilts I have designed for this book. These line drawings were made from my actual working drawings used in the creation of these quilts. In a couple of cases, I had to recreate the design from a photograph or from the quilt itself, and I simplified the design slightly. These charts will be easier to use if you enlarge them first at a photocopy shop.

The solid lines are design lines and the dotted lines are additional seam lines necessary to piece the quilts. Remember that if all four corners of a quilt are identical, you need draft only one corner full size. The templates necessary for each quilt have not been numbered, so you can apply your own numbering system to them. Remember that you need not make square or rectangular templates; they can be rotary cut directly from the fabric with Plexiglas square templates.

Where it is not obvious how a given design line was derived, place your ruler on that line and it will be obvious what two design points were used to create that line. Remember that not all end design points will be at the crossing of two design lines; some may be the center of a neighboring block or a neighboring shape, or perhaps an inch in (diagonally) from the corner of a shape.

If you compare the line drawings and their color photographs elsewhere in the book, you will understand how simple these designs really are. The complex look of these quilts often comes from strip piecing or cutting a single template out of two fabrics that have been previously sewn together. This latter process will allow you to strengthen certain shapes by outlining them on one edge with a second fabric.

For each quilt I have listed the quilt size (width × length) and the number and sizes of blocks its design accommodates. However, you can substitute blocks of different sizes if you redraw the quilt plan on a piece of eight-squares-per-inch graph paper, with your own grouping of blocks arranged in the center.

MARION'S FEATHERED FRIENDS

Photo on page 57
1999, collection of Marion Shelton Harlan, Everett, WA
Quilt Size: 64" × 64"
Number of Blocks: nine; four 10" × 10", five 8" × 8"

Design Notes: As you can see from the line drawing, there a number of ways of interpreting this design with value and color. Make several photocopies of this drawing and see how many variations you can come up with!

The pinwheels behind the blocks are all identical, but they are rotated a quarter turn as you go around the center block.

Piecing Notes: This is fairly complex piecing, but take your time and the final result will be worth it! Start with the shortest seams and work towards the longest ones. There are several places where you will need to use partial piecing.

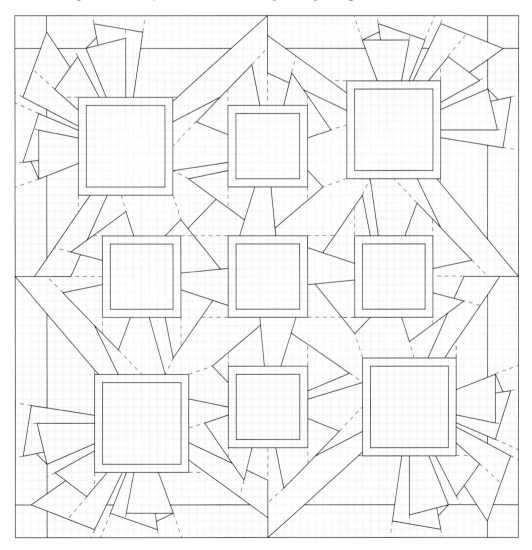

MARION'S STOREFRONTS

Photo on page 18
1992, collection of Marion Shelton Harlan, Everett, WA.
Quilt Size: 67" × 72"
Number of Blocks: fifteen; two 9" × 9" and thirteen 8" × 8"

Design Notes: After the blocks are sketched into the heart configuration, an additional border is drawn around each block. That border measures two inches wide in the interior of the heart shape, three inches wide on the outside. Where the borders cross each other, play with transparency. For example, if you alternate a light border around one block with a darker one around the next block, where the borders cross choose a fabric that is a value halfway between the light and the dark values. Or, if you have a red border around one block a blue one around its neighbor, use purples where the borders cross—just as you would if you were mixing paint.

Piecing Notes: In the "border within the border," the strip piecing can be random or regularly spaced, as shown.

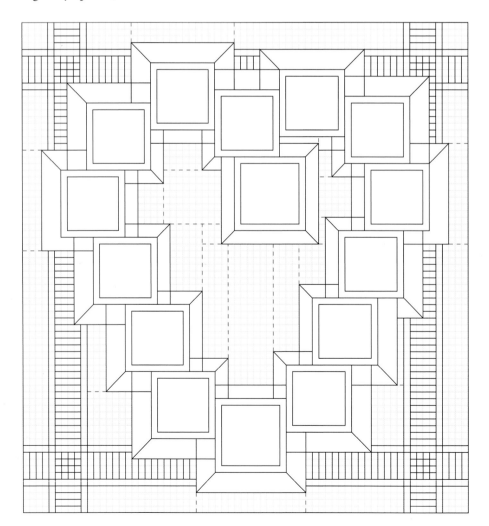

MARION'S FRIENDS I

Photo on page 10
1999, collection of Marion Shelton Harlan, Everett, WA
Quilt Size: 56" × 56"
Number of Blocks: seventeen; thirteen 6" × 6" and four 8" × 8"

Design Notes: Make a few photocopies of this line drawing to play with color placement. The border between the four corner blocks and the center block grouping can be interpreted a number of ways with various color and value placement.

Piecing Notes: Fairly easy to piece; watch your accuracy when sewing the long angles in the border.

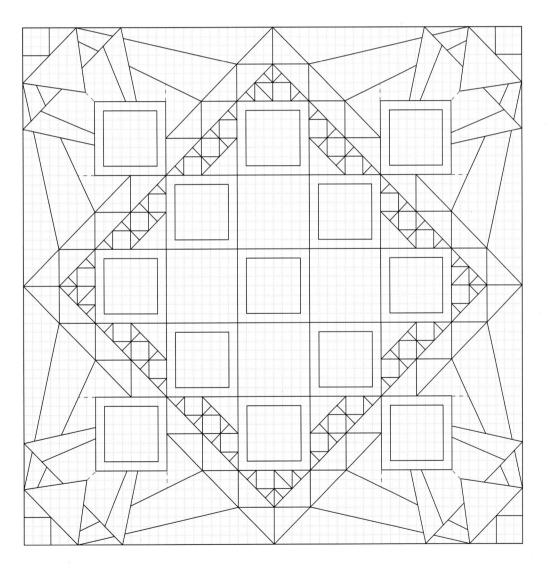

STARMAKER SERIES 1

Photo on page 23
1998, collection of Mary E. Hales, Mount Vernon, WA
Quilt Size: 39" × 58"
Number of Blocks: four; one 14" × 18" (with borders), two 8" × 8"
blocks on point, and one block was cut in half corner to corner and
placed on either side of the rectangular block

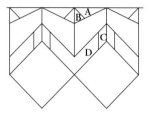

This border design has two places (shapes AB and CD) where joint templates can be used.

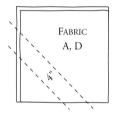

FABRIC A, D

Cut bias strips.

Design Notes: The zigzag border is made much more three-dimensional by using a lighter and a darker fabric, rather than a single fabric, in both the light beige and the gold zigzag behind it.

Piecing Notes: The star blocks can be made quickly by using speed methods of joining half-square triangles into squares. There are several places in this design where you can join two fabrics, then cut out a joint template.

Since template AB is at the edge of the quilt, it is important to place the side of the template at the edge of the quilt on the straight grain of the fabric. Template CD will be sewn to a bias edge, so its edges should be on straight grain too. To do this, cut bias strips 4" wide from fabrics A and D. Cut a bias strip 2" wide from fabric B and a straight grain strip of fabric 2" wide from fabric C. Sew fabrics A and B together, then sew fabrics C and D together, being careful not to stretch bias edges. Press. Place joint templates on joined fabrics as shown, aligning template design lines with seam lines on the joined fabrics.

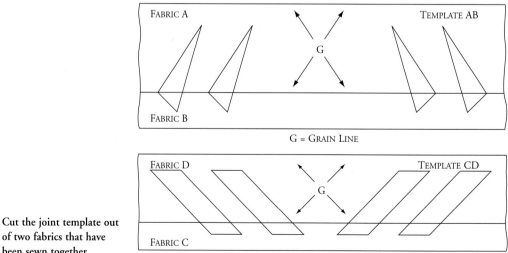

Cut the joint template out of two fabrics that have been sewn together.

EMPTY SPOOLS AT ASILOMAR III

Photo on page 24
1995, collection of Diana McClun, Walnut Creek, CA
Quilt Size: 72" × 81"
Number of Blocks: twenty-four, various sizes

Design Notes: The gold columns behind the blocks are very important; without them, it would look like I might as well have appliquéd these blocks onto a single background fabric.

There is no particular pathway for these offset blocks (circular, oval, heart-shaped, or serpentine); rather, they were offset in order to get as many blocks into this quilt as possible. Using a colored-paper blank to represent each block (with its border already attached) eliminated design anxiety about "which block goes where."

Note how unrelated in color and design these blocks are, and how that border around each one allows them all to exist happily in this quilt!

Piecing Notes: This quilt is very easy to piece, as it is made up largely of rectangles and squares. However, there is some partial piecing involved. The border is made of quarter-sections of the Jewel Box pattern.

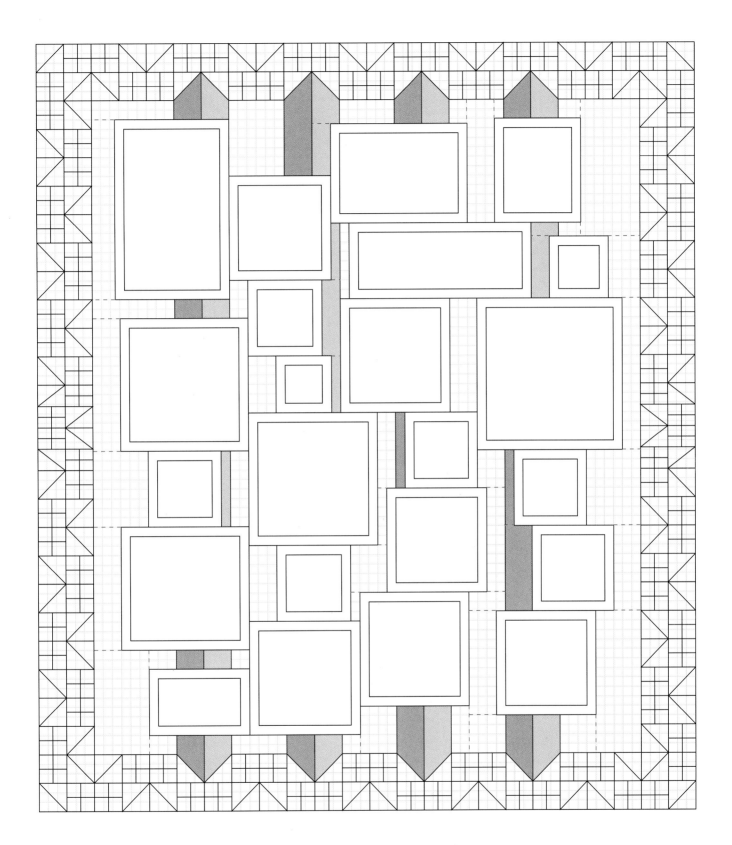

LIGHTHOUSES

Photo on page 43
1998, collection of Anne C. Smith, Gainesville, GA
Quilt Size: 64" × 84"
Number of Blocks: twenty, various sizes

Design Notes: Notice that most of the blocks are bordered in blue, but a few scattered throughout are bordered in red-orange. These red-orange borders draw the red-orange from the border into the center of the quilt.

Note that these blocks are offset from each other, but instead of touching each other, there is space in between. This space is not consistent as a standard sashing strip would be, but rather creates the feeling that the blocks are floating like oil droplets on water. The mechanism that gives them structure, that seems to keep them in place, is the innermost border. Since some of the blocks invade that border and others do not, a camouflaging of where the quilt stops and the border begins is achieved.

Piecing Notes: Relatively easy to piece, but partial piecing is necessary. Also, be as accurate as possible with the various angles in the border blocks.

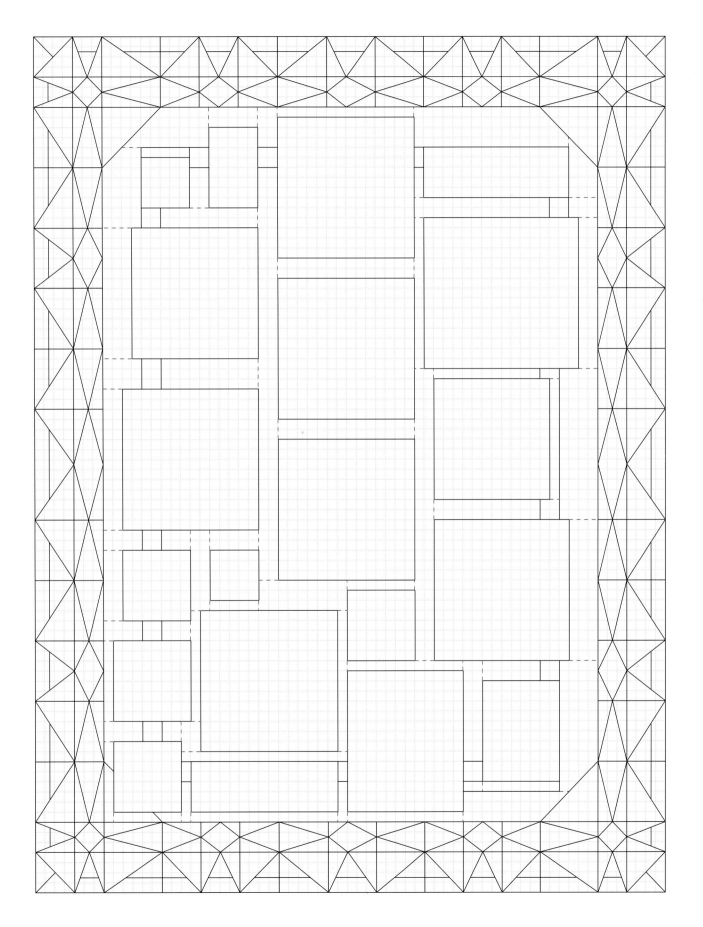

DON'T FENCE ME IN

Photo on page 52
1999, collection of Nancy J. Thorne, Merlin, OR
Quilt Size: 69" × 69""
Number of Blocks: eight 12" × 12" and numerous two-patch Rail Fence blocks

Design Notes: Make several photocopies of this line drawing and, in the open squares, play with various patterns you can make with the Rail Fence design. Use these patterns as a backdrop to the blocks (see Chapter Three, page 51–52). Notice that the "border within a border" was seamed down the middle to accommodate interesting use of a striped fabric.

Piecing Notes: Make the Rail fence blocks quickly as follows.

Cut numerous strips 2" × 22" (across the grain of the fabric; slit the fold opposite the selvages). Sew pairs of strips together, press seam.

Fold sewn strip in half, true up end (rotary cut across raw ends, cutting perpendicular to seam). Cut off 3¹/₂" segments to create the Rail Fence blocks.

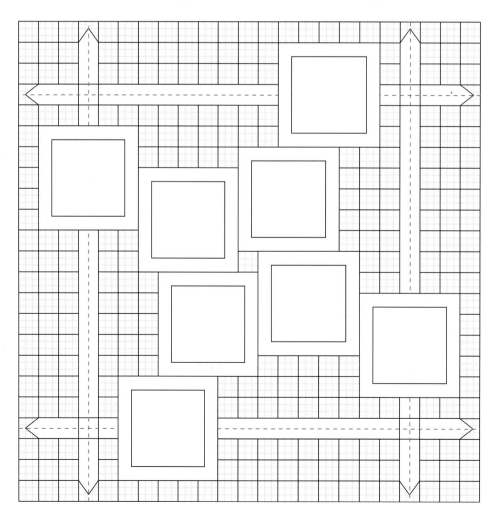

STARS OVER MEDORA

Photo on page 53
1999, collection of Dixie A. Whitmer, Bloomfield, MT
Quilt Size: 69" × 69"
Number of Blocks: Eight 12" × 12" and numerous two-patch Rail Fence

Design Notes: Make several photocopies of this line drawing to play with various patterns created with the Rail Fence blocks, as in *Don't Fence Me In*, page 52.

Piecing Notes: Very easy to piece. See piecing notes under *Don't Fence Me In*, page 78, for fast way to make many Rail Fence blocks.

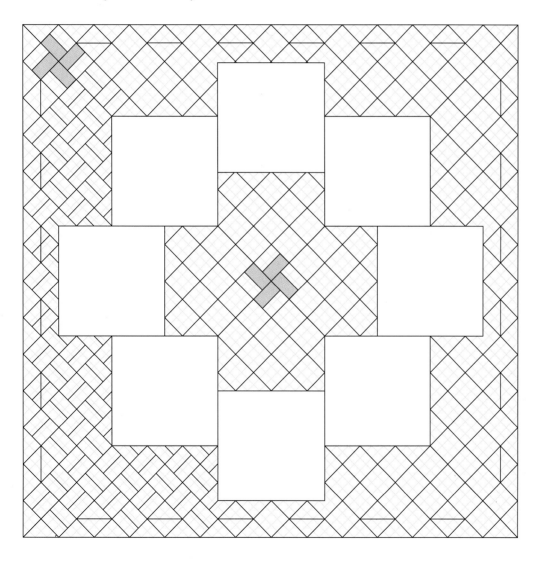

STARMAKER SERIES IV

Photo on page 29
1998, collection of Mary E. Hales, Mount Vernon, WA
Quilt Size: 66" × 66"
Number of Blocks: fifteen, various sizes

Design Notes: Two blocks were disassembled corner-to-corner to form the frame around the central feathered star block. Note how interesting the center of this quilt is because I changed the angle to create the lines surrounding the center block. The strip-pieced orange ribbons were the last shapes I cut before assembling the quilt top.

Piecing Notes: Fairly simple to piece; some partial piecing required.

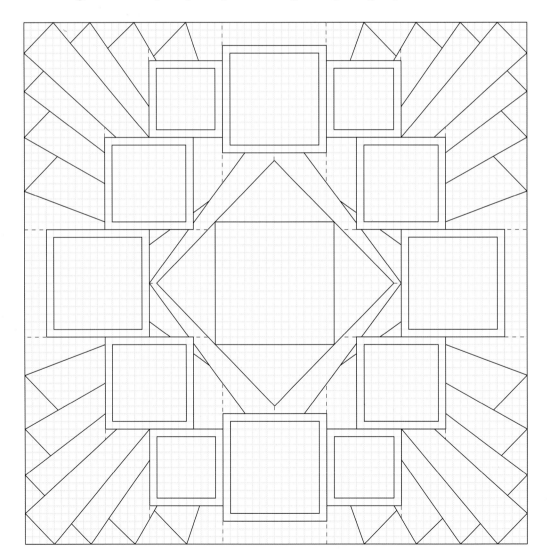

STARMAKER SERIES III

Photo on page 11
1998, collection of Mary E. Hales, Mount Vernon, WA
Quilt Size: 65" × 65"
Number of Blocks: seventeen; nine 12" × 12" and eight 8" × 8"

Design Notes: This is a fairly straightforward design; notice that some blocks are bordered, some are not.

Piecing Notes: There needed to be more textured areas of the quilt to transition between the pieced blocks and the background, so I strip pieced the light-to-medium blue shapes.

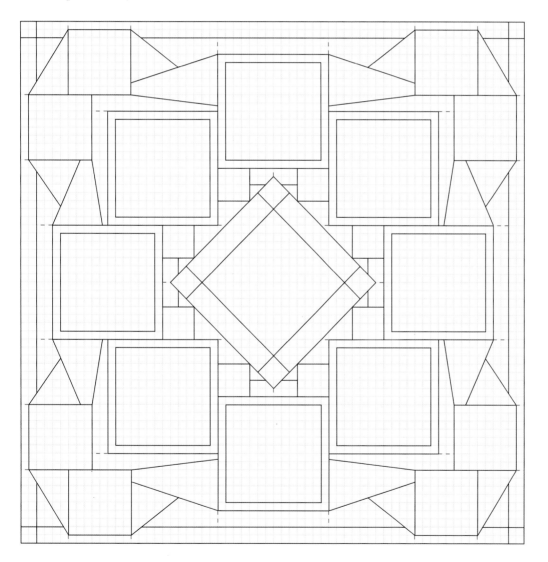

QUILTING BY THE LAKE SCHOLARSHIP FUND QUILT

Photo on page 57
1999, collection of Rebecca LaBarr, Oneonta, New York
Quilt Size: 58" × 58"
Number of Blocks: nine 12" × 12"; one was disassembled to make
four six inch blocks

Design Notes: I placed the two lightest-background blocks on the same side of the quilt as the lightest of the four "whirling triangles" in the background. If I had this quilt to design over again, I would break up those outermost elongated triangles even more than they are.

Piecing Notes: This is a quilt that needs care in the piecing because of the long seams at odd angles in some areas and very small pieces in others.

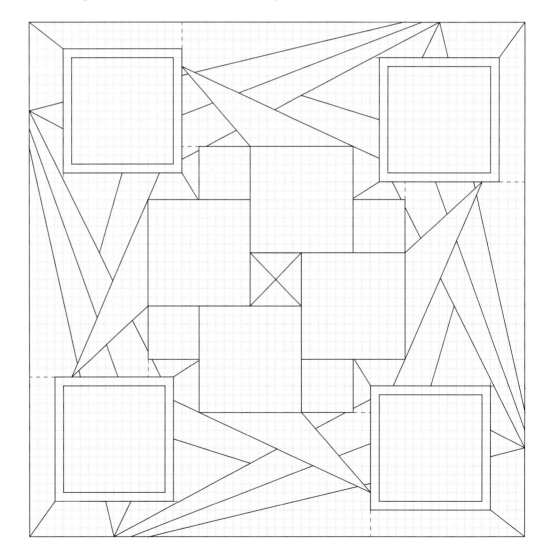

HORSIN' AROUND WITH THE SISTERS

Photo on page 30
1998, collection of Linda N. Gunby, Poulsbo, WA
Quilt Size: 64" × 66"
Number of Blocks: forty-four; one 12" × 14" center block, eight 12" × 12",
eight 6" × 6", four 3" × 3" nine-patches, and twenty-three 3" four-patches

Design Notes: This quilt draws the eye around the quilt with the little four-patch blocks. The border is not evenly divided. The first inner border is two units at one edge, six units at the other. The second and third borders are two units at one edge of the quilt and four units at the opposite edge.

Piecing Notes: Fairly easy to piece.

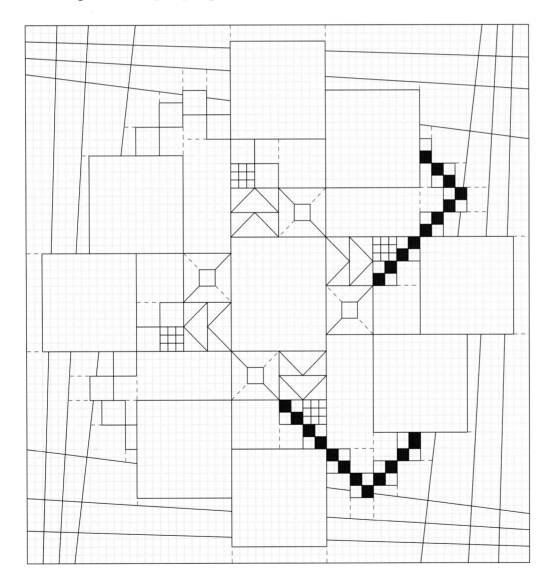

MEDORA ORANGE PEEL

Photo on page 42
1999, collection of Delores Cameron, Miles City, MT
Quilt Size: 62" × 62"
Number of Blocks: twelve 12" × 12"; three of which were disassembled for this layout

Design Notes: There are very few design lines that are not parallel to or at a 45 degree angle to the borders of this quilt. But these design lines are essential in softening this design. Variegated fabrics were used to build complexity into this design: the blue fabrics in the center make the medallion appear larger than it is. Also, the cloud fabric seems to blend right in to the light fabrics used in the corner blocks, though these fabrics are not related at all.

Piecing Notes: The Attic Window blocks on point around the center quilt square and the Rail Fence blocks linking the quilt squares around the center were originally one block. The lower right corner block was one of the original quilt squares as well; I removed one triangle from one corner of this block, then made three more similar blocks of related fabrics for the other corners.

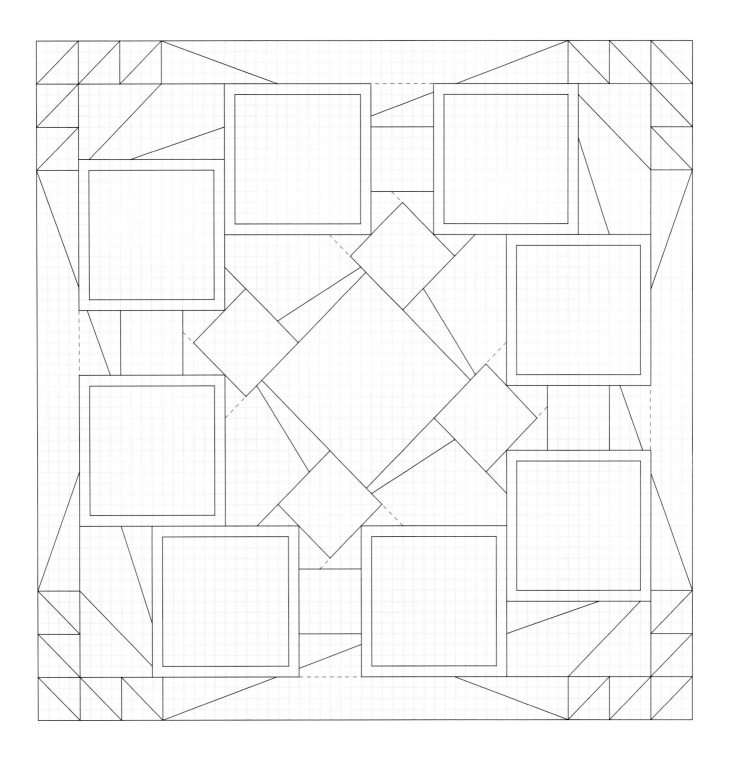

MEDORA ON MY MIND

Photo on page 15

1999, collection of Phyllis Bogart, Melnor, ND

Quilt Size: 66$^1/_2$" × 70"

Number of Blocks: twenty-three; one 10" × 10", eleven 12" × 12" (one of which was disassembled to make two rectangular single tree blocks), nine tree blocks the same size as the originals, and two additional trees in an abbreviated size to fit the quilt design

Design Notes: This was an adventure in arranging blocks in a regular format (blocks offset to form a circle around the center), then sprinkling the rectangular tree blocks throughout. Since the tree blocks blend into the background, the resulting design resembles blocks offset to form a spiral arrangement. There does not appear to be a formal border to this quilt; rather, there is a phantom Churn Dash block behind the quilt squares which appears to hold them all in place. Notice the low contrast between the stripe used in the border (which is arranged in a "north-south-east-west" linear orientation) and the stripe in the theme fabric for the blocks.

Piecing Notes: Fairly simple piecing; some partial piecing required.

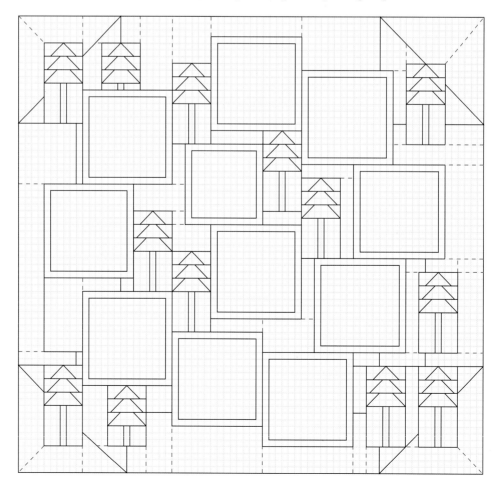

SISTERHOOD SPECIAL AND A SIDE OF STARS

Photo on page 46
1998, collection of Connie L. Tiegel, Atherton, CA
Quilt Size: 61" × 61"
Number of Blocks: forty-nine; one 12" × 12", eight 9" × 9",
twenty-four 4½" × 4½" stars, twelve 3" × 3" stars and four
corner blocks with borders (7½" by 9")

Design Notes: What makes this design especially appealing is "changing the angle" and interrupted lines. There is a nice balance of pieced and non-pieced (open) space.

Two different approaches to adding seam lines are presented in the drawing below. On the top and left sides are seam lines to use if you have a stripe and want to orient it perpendicular to the edges of the quilt. On the right and bottom sides is another seam line strategy for non-directional fabrics, which would be easier to piece, since there would not be so many set in corners.

Piecing Notes: Take care in piecing odd angles accurately.

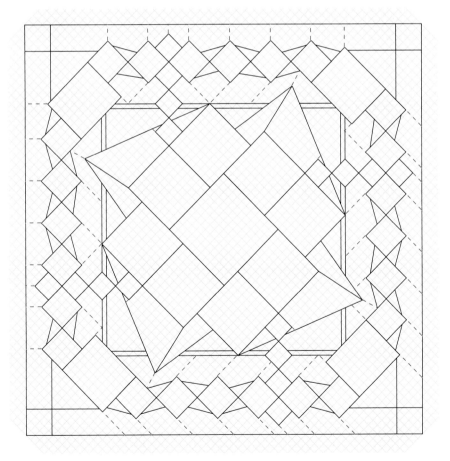

KERRY'S HEARTS I

Photo on page 14
1997, collection of Kerry I. Smith, Bainbridge Island, WA
Quilt Size: 70" × 70"
Number of Blocks: sixty-nine; one 12" × 14" rectangular center, thirty-two
6" × 6" (which appear to be different sizes because of different border widths
applied to them), thirty-six 4" × 4" flower blocks used to flesh out the ring
of blocks around the central medallion

Design Notes: This is a good example of how effective it is to use different size blocks in the same quilt. It is also a design that can accommodate both blocks straight and blocks on point. There is a high contrast between the background behind the twelve corner blocks, and the background behind the central ring of blocks. The use of blue variegated fabric brings excitement to a very simple border.

This quilt is a good example of using block segments to soften yet augment a design. The little flower-like pieced square (see two of them back-to-back above the top center quilt block) is actually a corner portion of a five-patch pattern called Cross and Crown. Note that these square block segments were "tucked in" where the blocks were offset from each other, just as baby's breath is tucked in to soften a bouquet of flowers.

Note the wide range of value (very light to very dark) and use of contrast in the background fabrics, which are used to suggest multiple "layers" of the quilt in which the blocks reside.

Piecing Notes: Because of the numerous seam angles and the amount of partial piecing required, this quilt is for intermediate to advanced quiltmakers.

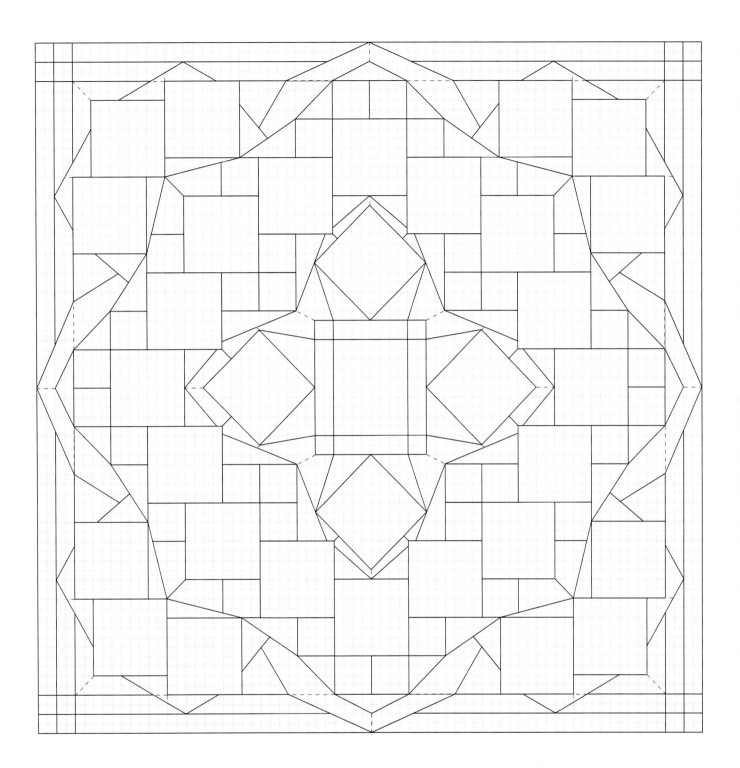

AFTERWORD

As I bring to a close this, my fifth book on quiltmaking, it feels right to reflect on where I am as a quiltmaker and writer at the end of one century and looking forward to adventures in the next one. I am struck by the thought that the real joy of quiltmaking comes not from winning awards, from finishing every quilt one begins, or even from the finishing of a given quilt project.

The real joy of quiltmaking is the *process* of it. We don't need quilts for our beds with central heating readily available; we don't need to hoard old clothing for fabrics with which to make quilts; most of us don't need to make quilts to earn a living or to be thrifty with fabric leftovers. We need to make quilts, and some of us need to write about it, because of the pure joy of the process.

That joy comes from:

- The feel of the fabric as we "see" it with our hands and fingers in the quilt shops and in our sewing rooms;
- The aroma of hot fabric as we press a seam;
- The sound of thread being drawn through two pieces of fabric;
- The "crisping up" of the design as we sew together the first few shapes from the design wall;
- The colors that dance into new combinations in our sewing rooms, either accidentally or purposefully;
- Watching a design progress on the design wall, no matter how frantic our daily schedules, and no matter how many transformations that design undergoes before its final version;
- Working, either alone in peace and quiet or with other women, some of whom are the most treasured of lifetime friends;
- The "energy factor"—no matter how tired we are from the activities of our day, if we can sew just one seam after supper is cleared away, we are able to sew long into the night;
- The pause in our day when we see something new and colorful emerge from the work of our hands;
- Making something beautiful or pleasing out of something as humble as a few small pieces of fabric;
- Having a reason to celebrate the work of other quiltmakers, no matter how simple or how grand their efforts.

And so, like you, dear reader, I look forward with great excitement to what the dawn of the new era will bring: new design ideas we will generate, new tools we will use, new ways we will find to rejoice in the process of quiltmaking.

APPENDIX A

Enlarge 198% to make 1¹/₂" square blocks.

APPENDIX B

Enlarge 142% to make 1½" square blocks.

RESOURCES/BIBLIOGRAPHY

RESOURCE LIST

The Cotton Patch Mail Order
3405 Hall Lane, Dept. CTB
Lafayette, CA 94549
E-mail: quiltusa@yahoo.com
Web: www.quiltusa.com
(800) 835-4418
(925) 283-7883
A Complete Quilting Supply Store

Omnigrid™
P. O. Box 663
Burlington, WA 98233
(800) 755-3530
All cutting products from this company are of the highest quality and accuracy. They are available at most good quilt shops and fabric stores, and through quilters' supply catalogs.

Kathy Sandbach
Custom Machine Quilting
22960 Shake Ridge Road
Volcano, CA 95689
E-mail: quiltlady@volcano.net
(209) 296-2298

Barbara Ford
Custom Machine Quilting
4858 N. Village Lane #B
Bellingham, Washington 98226
(360) 756-0317

Patsi Hanseth
Creative Machine Quilting
125 West Spruce Street
Mt. Vernon, WA 98273
(360) 336-3014

Mark Frey
Quilt Photographer
P. O. Box 1596
Yelm, WA 98597
(360) 894-3591

For more information on lectures and workshops by Margaret J. Miller, or to hire her to put some quilt blocks together for you, write to her at:
P. O. Box 798, Woodinville, WA 98072

BIBLIOGRAPHY

Beyer, Jinny. *The Quilter's Album of Blocks and Borders.* McLean, VA: EPM Publications, 1980.

Brackman, Barbara. *An Encyclopedia of Pieced Quilt Patterns.* Lawrence, KS: Prairie Flower Publishing, 1984.

Havig, Bettina. *Carrie Hall Blocks: Over 800 Patterns from the Collection Of the Spencer Museum of Art, University of Kansas.* Paducah, KY: American Quilter's Society, 1999.

Hopkins, Judy. *Around the Block with Judy Hopkins.* Bothell, WA: That Patchwork Place, Inc., 1994.

Martin, Judy. *Judy Martin's Ultimate Book of Quilt Block Patterns.* Denver, CO: Crosley-Griffith Publishing Company, 1988.

Martin, Judy. *The Block Book.* Grinnell, IA: Crosley-Griffith Publishing Company, Inc., 1998.

Miller, Margaret J. *Blockbender Quilts.* Bothell, WA: That Patchwork Place, Inc., 1995.

Miller, Margaret J. *Blockbuster Quilts.* Bothell, WA: That Patchwork Place, Inc., 1991.

McCloskey, Marsha. *Marsha McCloskey's Block Party.* Emmaus, PA: Rodale Press, Inc., 1998.

Thompson, Martha. *Square Dance: Fancy Quilts from Plain Squares.* Bothell, WA: That Patchwork Place, Inc., 1995.

INDEX

ABOUT *the* AUTHOR

Margaret J. Miller is a studio quiltmaker who travels widely, giving lectures and workshops on color and design that encourage students to reach for the unexpected in contemporary quiltmaking. Her full teaching schedule has taken her throughout the United States, as well as to Canada, Great Britain, Australia, New Zealand, South Africa, and Denmark. Her presentations are known for their enthusiasm, humor, and sincere encouragement of quiltmakers at all levels of skill and experience.

Having done various forms of needlework throughout her life, Margaret learned to quilt and applique in 1978. At that time, she was on the faculty of the Home Economics Department at California Polytechnic State University, San Luis Obispo, teaching a creative textiles class. She later moved to San Diego, where she started Tanglethread Junction, a pattern business featuring appliqué and stained glass appliqué designs. In 1982 she sold her business as part of her commitment to becoming a full-time quiltmaker.

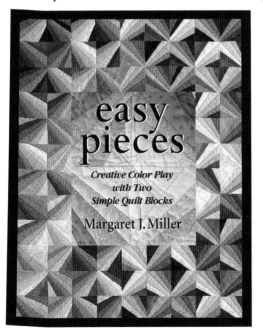

She now makes her home in her beloved Pacific Northwest, outside Seattle, Washington. There, her full life as a professional quiltmaker includes writing (this is her fifth book giving her unique perspective on the art and craft of quiltmaking), making quilts for one-woman shows and commissions, and keeping up with a killer travel schedule. Her skills as a gardener, another art she loves, are likely to stay at the "amateur but enthusiastic" level for quite a few years to come.

OTHER FINE BOOKS FROM C&T PUBLISHING

Appliqué 12 Easy Ways!: Charming Quilts, Giftable Projects & Timeless Techniques, Elly Sienkiewicz

Civil War Women: Their Quilts, Their Roles, and Activities for Re-Enactors, Barbara Brackman

Color From the Heart: Seven Great Ways to Make Quilts with Colors You Love, Gai Perry

Color Play: Easy Steps for Imaginative Color in Quilts, Joen Wolfrom

Diane Phalen Quilts: 10 Projects to Celebrate the Seasons, Diane Phalen

Easy Pieces: Creative Color Play with Two Simple Blocks, Margaret Miller

Exploring Machine Trapunto: New Dimensions, Hari Walner

Fabric Shopping with Alex Anderson, Seven Projects to Help You: Make Successful Choices, Build Your Confidence, Add to Your Fabric Stash, Alex Anderson

Fancy Appliqué: 12 Lessons to Enhance Your Skills, Elly Sienkiewicz

Fantastic Fabric Folding: Innovative Quilting Projects, Rebecca Wat

Freddy's House: Brilliant Color in Quilts, Freddy Moran

Free Stuff for Quilters on the Internet, 2nd Ed. Judy Heim and Gloria Hansen

From Fiber to Fabric: The Essential Guide to Quiltmaking Textiles, Harriet Hargrave

Hand Quilting with Alex Anderson: Six Projects for Hand Quilters, Alex Anderson

Heirloom Machine Quilting, Third Edition, Harriet Hargrave

Impressionist Palette, Gai Perry

Make Any Block Any Size, Joen Wolfrom

Mastering Quilt Marking: Marking Tools & Techniques, Choosing Stencils, Matching Borders & Corners, Pepper Cory

Patchwork Persuasion: Fascinating Quilts from Traditional Designs, Joen Wolfrom

Piecing: Expanding the Basics, Ruth B. McDowell

The Quilted Garden: Design and Make Nature-Inspired Quilts, Jane Sassaman

Quilting with the Muppets, The Jim Henson Company in Association with Sesame Television Workshop

Quilts from Europe, Projects and Inspiration, Gül Laporte

Rotary Cutting with Alex Anderson: Tips, Techniques, and Projects, Alex Anderson

Rx for Quilters: Stitcher-Friendly Advice for Every Body, Susan Delaney Mech, M.D.

Shadow Quilts: Easy to Design Multiple Image Quilts, Patricia Magaret and Donna Slusser

Start Quilting with Alex Anderson: Six Projects for First-Time Quilters, Alex Anderson

Trapunto by Machine, Hari Walner

Travels with Peaky and Spike: Doreen Speckmann's Quilting Adventures, Doreen Speckmann

The Visual Dance: Creating Spectacular Quilts, Joen Wolfrom

Wild Birds: Designs for Appliqué & Quilting, Carol Armstrong

Wildflowers: Designs for Appliqué & Quilting, Carol Armstrong

For more information write for a free catalog:
C&T Publishing, Inc.
P.O. Box 1456, Lafayette, CA 94549
(800) 284-1114
http://www.ctpub.com
e-mail: ctinfo@ctpub.com